The Abingdon Children's Sermon Library

Volume 1

The Abingdon Children's Sermon Library

Volume 1

Edited by
Brant D. Baker

Abingdon Press
Nashville

THE ABINGDON CHILDREN'S SERMON LIBRARY
VOLUME 1

Copyright © 2006 by Abingdon Press

All rights reserved.

This book is printed on acid-free paper.

Library of Congress Cataloging-in-Publication Data

The Abingdon children's sermon library / edited by Brant D. Baker.
  p. cm.
Includes index.
ISBN 0-687-49730-2 (pbk. : alk. paper)
1. Children's sermons. 2. Sermons, American. I. Baker, Brant D., 1958–

BV4315.A25 2006
252'.53—dc22

2005026092

06 07 08 09 10 11 12 13 14 15—10 9 8 7 6 5 4 3 2 1

MANUFACTURED IN THE UNITED STATES OF AMERICA

Contents

Contents

Contents

Contents

Introduction

Children are undeniably a gift from God. They give joy simply by virtue of the life that is in them, and their smiles can brighten the most somber face. Without even trying they bring innocent insight and uncomplicated understanding. They're not perfect, but they seem to know that and extend that acceptance to others as well.

Children in worship are undeniably a double gift from God. There are so many other places children, and their parents, can imagine being on Sunday mornings, and so to do something boring in that setting would be twice the loss. Biblical worship should be vibrant, enthusiastic, and filled with movement and sound.

Yet so often children's sermons are a lot like their adult counterparts—it really doesn't matter if anyone is there or not because there is no interaction, no exchange. Too many sermons, both adult and children's, are essentially a lecture that requires very little response from the hearer.

The book you are holding seeks to be a remedy, at least as far as children are concerned. Children (and most of us) do better with an active kind of listening. What we participate in, what we help create, holds the possibility of staying with us long enough to transform us. In the sermons that follow, the children are active participants and co-creators—there could be no sermon without the hearers because they are part of the action and part of the message. Along the way the children, the congregation, and the leader all discover that being in God's holy house not only fulfills our obligation and need to worship, but also blesses us in joy.

This collection of fifty-two children's sermons is set up to be used over a calendar year and so begins with New Year and ends at Christmas. All of the main liturgical and nonliturgical holidays are covered, together with many sermons that could be used any time. A Scripture index at the back will be of additional help in choosing a sermon appropriate for the day's preaching text. Permission is given to reproduce pages from this book to use as a guide for the leader and helpers, provided the following credit line and copyright notice appear on all copies: From *The Abingdon Children's Sermon Library, Volume 1*. Copyright © 2006 by Abingdon Press.

While a brief outline in hand can be helpful, and while lengthy and complex sections of narrative may require more elaborate notes, the children's sermon leader really needs to be familiar with the outline and flow of the sermon for the day. Reading these sermons outright would be a travesty! Spontaneity and unpredictability are hallmarks of children's sermons, and leaders of these events need to be comfortable with these distractions. And, since no two groups of children will give the same responses, looking for your sermon to flow exactly as ours do is futile. The well-prepared leader will know generally where the sermon is headed and will therefore be able to receive the sometimes wondrously tangential comments and questions of the children without panic. Similarly, silence need not create a crisis: the leader should feel free to suggest answers that are not otherwise forthcoming, or even to ask the congregation to supply the answer (just to be sure they are listening). The bottom line is that leaders (1) should know their material well enough to take it where it needs to go, and (2) should have fun!

Children in worship are a wonderful gift. May you be blessed as you bring them into the awe and wonder of our great and glorious God.

Last-Minute Children's Sermon

It never fails. You've planned your week, scheduling an hour on Thursday morning to work on the children's sermon, and then you get called to the hospital for a situation that lasts into Saturday night. Or, you make all the arrangements for one of the wonderful sermons in this book and on Sunday morning show up to find that your helper is sick in bed. Or, you ask someone else to lead the children's sermon; but when the time comes in the service, they just give you a blank stare. You then realize that you intended to ask them, but something else happened and you never got around to it.

This children's sermon is for just such times as these. Tuck this away in your Bible, and then try to forget you have it until you really need it!

Leader: Good morning, it's great to see everyone today. Instead of going on some big adventure today, I thought we might just talk. And I wonder if any of you have any questions for me?

Children: (*May or may not have any. If so, enjoy answering them. If not . . .*)

L: Well then, I have some questions for you:
Why did God make giraffes and anteaters?
How many ticklish spots do you have? Why?
Did Jesus like to laugh?
Does Jesus love you? How do you know?
We know God loves us because he made giraffes, anteaters, ticklish spots, and every other good thing in our lives. Jesus loves us and loves life and loves laughter! Let's say a prayer and thank Jesus for all that and more . . . (*prayer*).

—*Brant D. Baker*

Our God Reigns

Scripture: Isaiah 52:7; Isaiah 43:19

Season/Sunday: Any, but this sermon could work well for the Sunday closest to New Years by including reference to Isaiah's proclamation of God doing a new thing (Isaiah 43:19).

Focus: Bringing the Good News of God's coming reign.

Experience: The children will pretend they are messengers of old, running through the mountains with a wonderful message to share.

Arrangements: None are needed, although wearing a pair of running shoes and making an entrance from the back of the church (the narthex) would be a nice touch. To make such an entrance might mean an assistant would call the children forward. Note: if movement around the sanctuary is impractical or impossible, leader may want to lead the children in running in place and "pretending" the route.

Leader: (*Jogging up from whatever entry point is possible and pretending (?!) to be out of breath.*) Wow, I'm out of breath! You see, I've been thinking hard about the way the messengers in the old days sometimes had to run from one place to the other to share their news. Some of those messengers were called "prophets"; and one of those prophets, named Isaiah, talks about taking his message across the mountains. Hey, I've got an idea! Let's pretend to be a prophet like Isaiah, running up and down the mountains, proclaiming our message. Are you ready to run?

Children: Yes!

L: Okay, let's start running up this mountain right here (*make your way up one of the aisles*). Oh, it's a big mountain (*look like you're running hard up a hill—*

2

of course, you may be!). Now let's go across this valley (*turning and going across the back of the sanctuary*). And finally, let's go right down (*insert name of road or street on which the church is located or some commonly known geological feature of your area*). And here we come to the sanctuary of (*church name*) church, and here (*with excitement in your voice*), and here are God's people! Are you ready to proclaim good news to God's people like Isaiah?

C: Yes!

L: Okay, everybody repeat after me. "Your God reigns!"

C: "Your God reigns!"

L: "My God reigns!"

C: "My God reigns!"

L: "Jesus Christ is our God!"

C: "Jesus Christ is our God!"

L: "Jesus Christ reigns!"

C: "Jesus Christ reigns!"

L: "Let us praise the Lord!"

C: "Let us praise the Lord!"

L: "Amen."

C: "Amen."

L: Let's have our prayer and be thankful for the good news that God does reign in this place . . . (*prayer*).

—*Bob Sharman*

God's Messenger

Scripture: Malachi 3:1, 1:2

Season/Sunday: Any

Focus: The big message here is about little prophets giving a big word!

Experience: Delivering a message to God's people.

Arrangements: None are needed, although you may want to think through how best to guide the children in coming up with the message they are to deliver. One choice is to use Malachi 1:2 (as is done below) or another verse of scripture appropriate to the day. Another option is to create your own message such as, "God is here right now and wants to bless each of you." If there is time and the children are a little older, and you are feeling adventurous, the children could be asked to huddle and actually think about something they think God would like to say to the congregation. Such an approach has its advantages and its pitfalls, and you would probably want to have one of the first two options ready in case this did not work out. Nevertheless, who knows but that God would say something important indeed through the voices of these young prophets!

Leader:	Good morning! Great to see everyone because today I want to introduce you to someone who has a very unusual name. His name was Malachi. Can you say that with me?
Children:	Malachi.
L:	Can you guess what his name means in the Hebrew language?
C:	Malachi. Mal-guy? A kind of bread?
L:	Those are interesting guesses, but the real meaning of Malachi's name is "messenger." Can you imagine being named "Messenger"? "Hello, Messenger!" "How was your day today, Messenger?" "Hey, Messenger, can you take a message?"

C: (*giggles*)

L: Well, that was Malachi's name, and it also was what he did for God. He was a messenger for God. Here's what it says in Malachi 3:1 (NIV): "See, I will send my [Malachi] messenger, who will prepare the way before me." So Malachi was a messenger who was sent by God to prepare the way. What does a messenger do for God?

C: He tells people about God. He tells them what God wants.

L: I think you are all exactly right. Malachi was a messenger that God sent to give a message to God's people. Say, do you suppose we could all be messengers for God today? Let's stand up and give God's people here in our church a message, and we can borrow one from Mr. Messenger. Come here and huddle up with me, and we'll learn our message before we give it.

C: (*huddle*)

L: (*In a quiet voice teach the children Malachi 1:2, "'I have loved you,' says the* LORD*." Then stand up and deliver together in a loud voice.*)

C: "'I have loved you,' says the LORD."

L: Good job, everyone! Messages are fun to give, aren't they? Let's bow our heads and give thanks for God's messengers and important messages . . . (*prayer*).

—*Bob Sharman*

The Getaway

Scripture: Jonah 1:3, 2:7

Season/Sunday: Any

Focus: This sermon looks at God's constant presence with us, even when we're trying to get away.

Experience: Running away from God and being found by God.

Arrangements: A poster board with the word TARSHISH in large, colorful letters, to be held by an assistant such as a teenager or one of the ushers.

Leader:	Okay everybody, you're not going to believe this! You're just not going to believe what I have read in the Bible. This comes from the prophet named Jonah. Can everyone say Jonah?
Children:	Jonah!
L:	Right, Jonah. But you're not going to believe what this prophet Jonah did. The Bible says that "Jonah ran away from the LORD and headed for Tarshish" (Jonah 1:3, NIV). Can you believe that? Can you believe Jonah ran away from the Lord to a place called Tarshish? What about you—have you ever run away to Tarshish?
C:	Nooo!
L:	Well I certainly hope not! Have any of you ever run away from some <u>one</u>?
C:	Yes. No. I ran away from a boy at school this week.
L:	I'll tell you what, lets pretend we're Jonah and that we're going to run away from God. Do you think we can make it to Tarshish?
C:	No!
L:	Well, we might. Why, just look back there! (*Leader points to the back of the sanctuary where the assistant is holding the sign that says "Tarshish."*) There's

6

Tarshish right there, so let's get running! (*Leader runs with children to "Tarshish."*)

(*Upon arrival*) Okay, and just to be sure we got away, let's all get down and see if we can hide from God.

C: (*giggles*)

L: Well, what do you think—have we been able to run away from God?

C: No, we're still in the sanctuary!

L: (*standing up*) That's right! We can't hide from God in the sanctuary, and we can't hide from God anywhere. Jonah couldn't run away from God either. In fact, Jonah wrote in his book:

When my life was ebbing away,
(that's when he had run away)
I remembered you, LORD,
and my prayer rose to you. (Jonah 2:7, NIV)

Jonah found out that God was with him wherever he went. That's good news. And when Jonah discovered this, he lifted a prayer to God.

Let's be like Jonah and lift our hands high to the Lord and give thanks that wherever we go, God is with us . . . (*prayer*).

—*Bob Sharman*

God's Great Deeds

Scripture: Habakkuk 3:2

Season/Sunday: Any

Focus: This sermon looks at God's great deeds in the Bible, and in your church!

Experience: Remembering those deeds, imagining deeds God may yet want to do, believing God can do great deeds in our midst, and praying for just that.

Arrangements: A Bible with the book of Habakkuk marked.

Leader: Hello everyone. Has anyone ever heard of the prophet Habakkuk? Can you say it with me? Ha-<u>bak</u>-kuk.

Children: Habakkuk!

L: I'm not surprised you haven't heard of him. Habakkuk's book in the Bible is only three pages long, look (*show Bible opened to book of Habakkuk*). But his words are very important. Listen,

LORD, I have heard of your fame;
  I stand in awe of your deeds, O LORD.
Renew them in our day,
  in our time make them known. (Habakkuk 3:2, NIV)

What do you suppose Habakkuk means when he says he has heard of the famous deeds of the Lord? What famous deeds has God done? Can you think of any?

C: *(Various answers, some biblical, some extra-biblical, some implausible!)*

L: Okay, now the most important question is: Do you think God can do great and famous deeds again? In fact, do you think the Lord can do great and famous deeds in our church?

C: Yes. No.

L: What kinds of great deeds can God do in our church?

C: Miracles. Make it so there are more cookies at snack time. Make more people come. Close the church so that I won't have to come any more.

L: Wow, some interesting answers there! Well, God *has* done great things, and God most certainly can do great things for our church too, especially if we ask like Habakkuk did for God to renew those deeds in our day. Let's stand up and have a prayer, and pretend we're Habakkuk. Will you repeat this prayer after me?

Lord, we have heard of your fame *(echo)*;
we stand in awe of your deeds *(echo)*.
Renew them here at *(name of church)* *(echo)*;
we ask you to do mighty things *(echo)*.

> *(If the children mentioned as one of their hoped for "mighty deeds" a particular activity in the life of the church, it would be wonderful to lift this desire up in prayer.)*

Jesus we believe you can do these things *(echo)*.
Surprise us, we pray, with your awesome power *(echo)*,
for we give our church to you *(echo)*.
We pray in Jesus' name; amen *(echo)*.

—*Bob Sharman*

The Call of God (One)

Scripture: Mark 12:28-31

Season/Sunday: Any

Focus: Understanding the many ways God calls people can be difficult, even for adults. While introducing the notion that God calls us to specific tasks and ministries, this sermon is really designed to help children explore the *general* call of God to love, serve, obey, and worship.

Experience: The sermon will be continually interrupted by cell phone calls (*hopefully not a common problem in your worship!*), which will set up the teaching content.

Arrangements: You will need a number of cell phones (*three would be about right, stuck in various pockets in your clothes*) and a helper who will call you on each one in turn as you are trying to get started in talking about "the call of God." It might help for the caller to put the numbers into his or her own cell phone's speed dial (*you may have to ad-lib a bit if the calls don't come through right on cue*). A short practice beforehand would be a good idea. You should also have a Bible with you.

> **Leader:** Good morning, it's great to see everyone! Today we're going to talk for a few minutes about the call of God (*cue for first cell phone to ring*). . . . Oh, uh, I'm so sorry; let me just get that. (*Answering phone*) Hello. Yes, well, I'm sorry I can't really talk right now, okay. . . . Sorry, now about the call of God. In the Bible God sometimes comes to people and asks them to do special things, and that's a call . . . (*second phone rings*).
>
> **Children:** (*laughter*)
>
> **L:** Hello, oh hi. Well, I'm a little busy at the moment. How'd you get this number anyway? Never mind; I'll talk to you later.

Okay, where were we? Oh yeah, the call of God.
Sometimes in the Bible stories God comes as an
angel, or sends a messenger to call people . . . (*third
phone rings*). Oh, my goodness! I am <u>so</u> sorry!
Hello? No, this isn't Joe's Pizza! Good bye! Boy,
that's so distracting; . . . what were we talking about?

C: The call of God! (*You should be sure to make children recall this—they should have it by now!*)

L: Oh right! Now, seriously, does God ever call us on
the phone?

C: No!

L: No? Are you sure? Do you know what God's cell
phone looks like? (*Bring hands together in a posture
of prayer.*)

C: Oh!

L: Or, God's cell phone sometimes looks like this (*pick
up Bible*). Or even sometimes, God speaks to us
through events or other people. And even if God isn't
calling us to something specific every single moment,
God is always calling us to worship Jesus Christ and
to love and serve other people. Let's have a prayer
and give thanks that God calls us to do so many
wonderful and interesting things . . . (*prayer*).

—*Brant D. Baker*

The Call of God (Two)

Scripture: 1 Samuel 3:1-10

Season/Sunday: Any

Focus: The call of God is a unique and individual thing. The focus of this sermon is to affirm that we may hear God calling our hearts when we least expect it.

Experience: To have someone in the congregation call the name of one of the children three times, to send the child to investigate, but to find no one to identify as the speaker.

Arrangements: You will want to arrange for the "Caller," being sure to explain the flow of the sermon and to agree on one of the children whose name will be called out. A double check before the service begins to verify that the child is indeed present (or a call to the parents the night before!) would be wise.

> **Leader:** Well hello! How is everyone today? Great to see you, and it's good that you all are here because we have something very important to talk about . . . (*cue to caller*).
>
> **Caller:** Christopher!
>
> **L:** What was that?
>
> **Children:** Someone called Christopher!
>
> **L:** (*Turning to Christopher*) Christopher, who would be calling you?
>
> **Christopher:** I don't know!
>
> **L:** Well, you better go see so that we can continue (*child goes out into congregation*).
>
> **Christopher:** Who called me?
>
> **L:** Well, Christopher, come on back, and we'll keep going. Now let's see, I said "good morning," and then I said we had something important to talk about, and . . .
>
> **Caller:** Christopher!!
>
> **Christopher:** Oh, brother!

L: Go ahead, see if you can find out who called.

Christopher: No one says they did it!

L: Oh well, let's keep going. The important thing I want to talk to you about this morning is in the Bible and . . .

Caller: CHRISTOPHER!

Christopher: I know, I know, go and see who it is.

L: Well, you know, this has worked out pretty well anyway, because I wanted to tell you this morning about Samuel. He was a young man, serving in the temple, and he kept hearing his name called. He thought it was the priest, but who do you think it turned out to be?

C: God? Jesus?

L: That's right. Sometimes God can call us, and speak, maybe not with a voice that we hear like Christopher heard; but God can speak to our hearts. Let's have a prayer and give thanks that God sometimes calls our hearts and tells us how much we are loved . . . *(prayer)*.

—Brant D. Baker

Manna from Heaven

Scripture: Exodus 16:1-16

Season/Sunday: Any

Focus: God provides for our every need, even when we do not expect it, sometimes in the least likely places and most unusual ways.

Experience: To follow Moses into the wilderness and hear the grumbling of the people, to get a chance to grumble ourselves, and then to experience God's manna from heaven.

Arrangements: You will need wrapped cookies or candy that the choir or some other group can toss out to the children. If your church prohibits eating in the sanctuary, give the children a gentle reminder at the end of the sermon to enjoy their snack later. If your choir is not in a location convenient for this, pick another section of the congregation and give them the treats and instructions beforehand.

Also you will need to prepare several members of the congregation to be the complainers, with lines such as, *"We're hungry! When are we going to get something to eat?" "Are we there yet?" "I want to go back to Egypt! At least we had something to eat back there!"*

Finally, as the children come forward, invite the congregation to help with this sermon. Instruct them to be ready to grumble on cue. Practice the "grumbling" once or twice so they will get into the spirit of things.

Leader:	Good morning! Today we're going to remember the story of Moses as he led the people of God in the wilderness. Have you ever been on a trip where it took a really long, long, long, long, long, long, long time to get to?
Children:	Yeah! We rode in the car for hours and hours!
L:	Did you like riding in the car so long? Did you get grumpy?

14

C: Yes. No.

L: Let's pretend we're the people of God, and we are going to follow Moses on a long journey. Come on (*start a long slow journey around the sanctuary*). The people of God had to go on a long, long, long trip once. When God freed them from being slaves in Egypt, they had to find a new home. So they were traveling to their new home that God had promised. They had to travel through a pretty tough place called the wilderness. Do you know what they felt like sometimes?

C: Were they hungry? Did they get bored? How much farther is it?

L: Yep. They wondered if they were ever going to get there. And they got hungry, and tired, and cranky. They began to grumble (*cue the congregation to start grumbling*) . . . and grumble . . . and complain about everything (*cue the complainers*).

Complainers: "We're hungry! When are we going to get something to eat?" "Are we there yet?" "I want to go back to Egypt! At least we had something to eat back there!"

L: (*Stopping in front of the designated spot where manna is to appear. Preferably the children will have their backs to the group that will toss the manna.*) Then Moses prayed to the Lord, and God said, "I have heard their complaining." And God promised to give them something to eat. Do you know what God gave them to eat?

C: McDonald's? A sandwich?

L: God gave them manna (*cue for the manna to be tossed gently out over to the children*).

C: Cookies!

L: One morning, there on the surface of the wilderness, after the dew had lifted they saw a white flaky substance that looked like frost. They could eat it. It was called manna, and your cookies this morning are to remind us of how God provided for the people when they were hungry. Let's have a prayer and thank God for all God's good things . . . (*prayer*).

—*Jeff Hutcheson*

Growing Up to Be Like Jesus

Scripture: Ephesians 4:15

Season/Sunday: Any

Focus: This sermon looks at role models in our lives and suggests that Jesus is the perfect One we would want to be like when we grow up.

Experience: To identify with various types of role models in our lives.

Arrangements: None are needed, but have a good grasp of the types of people you will want to suggest to the children (sports heroes, super-heroes, and family members are used in the sermon below). The tendency of the children will be to think about <u>what</u> they want to be when they grow up, and it may take some careful prompting to redirect their thinking to the question of <u>who</u> they want to be like.

> **Leader:** Who do you want to be like when you grow up? This isn't the same question as "What do you want to be when you grow up?" What I want to know is if you've thought about <u>who</u> you want to be like when you grow up. Let's see, I'm thinking about . . . sports figures. Does anyone here want to grow up to be like Randy Johnson, or Curt Schilling, or Steve Nash, or maybe even Tiger Woods *(substitute sports figures from your own hometown as applicable)*? If you want to grow up to be like someone in sports, stand up!
>
> **Children:** *(A few stand.)*
>
> **L:** Who?
>
> **C:** *(Name some sports figures.)*
>
> **L:** And congregation, let's ask you the same thing: if any of you wanted to be like a sports hero as you were growing up, would you please stand?

16

Congregation: *(A few stand.)*

L: And let's hear who you had in mind *(call on a few to name their hero).* Okay, let's sit back down, and now . . . oh, I know, super-heroes! Do any of you want to grow up to be like Wonder Woman or Spiderman? If you do, stand up!

C: *(A few stand—ask them who they want to be like.)*

L: And congregation, any of you who wanted to grow up to be like a super-hero? *(A few stand—solicit names.)* That's great! Okay, let's sit down. And now I'm thinking about . . . oh! Who wants to grow up to be like your mom, or your dad, or maybe a grandparent or aunt or uncle . . . ? If you want to grow up to be like a family member, stand up!

C: *(Quite a few stand, ask them who they are thinking about.)*

L: That's great; and congregation, if you wanted to be like a family member as you grew up, would you please stand *(many do).*

Okay, now let me ask you one last question. If you want to grow up to be like <u>Jesus</u>, would you please stand? *(All stand.)* That's right, we all want to be like Jesus when we grow up, and that's what God wants too. The Bible says that we should all grow up into Christ (Ephesians 4:15). That way we can be like the One sent to show us what God had in mind for human life! Let's have a prayer and give thanks that we have such a good role model in Jesus . . . *(prayer).*

—*Brant D. Baker*

Peace! Be Still! Even the Sea and Wind Obey Him

Scripture: Mark 4:35-41

Season/Sunday: Any

Focus: During our stormy and scary times we should hold fast to our faith in Jesus. He is always there to protect us and give us peace.

Experience: The children will relive the scripture passage using various props.

Arrangements: You will need a set of noisemakers such as tambourines, triangles, drumsticks, and shakers (*you can make shakers with soda cans and rice!*), but not every child needs one. You will need a large piece of cloth, preferably dark blue or black to represent the rough seas. Place all these props in a bag. An adult helper is recommended to guide the children through the reenactment.

Leader: Good morning! I hope everyone is doing great today, but . . . I was wondering, have you ever been scared before?

Children: Yes, one time when the lightening came. My brother scared me.

L: Yeah, me too. Well, this morning I want to tell you about a time when Jesus' disciples were scared, and I need all of you to help me with the story. (*Bring out the bag of props.*) OK, let me see what I have in this bag to help us (*take out the large cloth*). Would some of you spread out around this cloth and smooth it out on the floor?

C: (*Helper and children smooth out the cloth.*)

L: Let's see what else we've got in here (*take out the instruments and begin distribution*). If you take one of these, you'll have to watch me and listen carefully to the instructions I give you during the story, OK?

C: OK!

L: I think we're ready to tell the story together. The story is from the New Testament in the gospel of Mark, chapter 4, verses 35-41. One evening, after a long day of teaching, Jesus said to his disciples, "Let us go across to the other side." So leaving the crowd behind, they took him with them in the boat. Children, let's pretend we're in the boat.

C: (*Leader and children rock back and forth gently.*)

L: The sea was very gentle, so let's pick up the cloth and wave the cloth gently. Keep waving it gently until I tell you to stop!

C: (*Helper and children pick up the cloth and create gentle waves with the cloth. After a few seconds of waving . . .*)

L: Uh oh, do you hear that? The wind is picking up. Children with the instruments, make gentle and slow noises with your instruments—not too loud, as quietly and slowly as you can. And don't stop until I tell you to stop!

C: (*Children play their instruments gently and slowly.*)

L: As the night went on, the winds got stronger (*signal to the children to make their instruments louder*) and the waves got bigger and bigger (*signal to the children to make the waves with the cloth bigger*). The waves got so big; the water beat into the boat. The disciples were scared. Children show me your scared faces.

C: (*Children show their scared faces.*)

L: The disciples were very scared. They wondered, "Where is Jesus?" They looked around and found Jesus asleep in the back of the boat. They said to Jesus, "Teacher, do you not care that we are in danger?" Jesus woke up and told the wind to stop, and said to the sea, "Peace! Be Still!" Then the wind stopped. (*Signal to the children to stop playing the instruments.*) There was a dead calm in the sea. (*Signal to the children to stop waving the cloth and flatten it.*) Jesus said to the disciples, "Why are you afraid? Have you still no faith?" The disciples were filled with great awe and said to one another, "Who then is this, that even the wind and the sea obey him?" Now, children, give me your peaceful faces.

C: (*Children make peaceful faces.*)

L: Wow, that was scary. Good thing Jesus was there to command the wind and the sea to stop. Good job, everyone, for helping me tell the story. I hope that the next time you're scared, you'll remember this story and you'll remember that Jesus is watching over you. Let's have a prayer and thank God that Jesus can give us peace when we are scared . . . *(prayer).*

—*Joyce S. Fong*

Jesus Says—"I Am"

Scripture: The "I Am" statements of Jesus from John 6:35, 8:12, 10:1, and 14:6

Season/Sunday: Any

Focus: The "I Am" statements of Jesus help us to understand the many ways Jesus meets our needs. In this sermon the children will get an overview of all of these profound statements.

Experience: Children will play a true/stand–false/sit game based upon their familiarity with the "I Am" statements of Jesus. Children will stand or stay seated in response to various statements offered by the leader. As the game progresses increase the speed and make your delivery more energetic.

Arrangements: No special arrangements are needed, but you may want to carry a copy of this sermon with you to help you remember the quotations.

Leader: Let's play a game this morning. In the Bible, Jesus calls himself by many different names. Let's see how many you might know. If you think it's true, that Jesus said it, stand up. If you think he didn't say it, stay seated. Got it? Stand up for yes, keep sitting for no. Did Jesus say, "I am the cheese fondue"?

Children: (*Children should remain seated—you hope!*)

L: No, everyone should have stayed seated. . . . Jesus never said he was the cheese fondue. Here's our next one, "I am the bread of life."

C: (*Children should stand up.*)

L: That's right, we should stand for that one; Jesus did say, "I am the bread of life. Whoever comes to me will never be hungry" (John 6:35). All right, you get the idea. Sit back down and let's go a little faster. . . . Did Jesus say, "I am the cat's meow"?

C: (*Remain seated.*)

L: No, Jesus never said that. How about, "I am the light of the world"?

C: (*Stand.*)

L: Yep, Jesus did say that he was the light of the world and whoever follows him will not live in darkness (John 8:12). All right, sit back down. (*Speeding up*) Did Jesus say, "I am the bologna sandwich"?

C: (*Remain seated.*)

L: No, that's silly, Jesus never said that. . . . Did he say, "I am the way, and the truth, and the life"?

C: (*Stand.*)

L: Yes, Jesus did say that he was "the way, and the truth, and the life," and that "no one comes to the Father" but through him (John 14:6). Okay, sit back down. These are the last ones, so who wants to go really fast?

C: Me!

L: Did he say, "I am the Happy Meal"?

C: (*Remain seated.*)

L: How about "I am the magic carpet"?

C: (*Remain seated.*)

L: What about "I am the great rabbit"?

C: (*Remain seated.*)

L: What about "I am the good shepherd"?

C: (*Stand.*)

L: Yes, Jesus said, "I am the good shepherd. The good shepherd lays down his life for the sheep" (John 10:11). Jesus tells us that he is many things that are helpful to us—the bread of life; the light of the world; the way, the truth, and the life; and the good shepherd. Let's pray and thank Jesus for being so many different things to help us, protect us, and love us . . . (*prayer*).

—Benjamin Keller

The Wall Came Tumbling Down

Scripture: Joshua 6:1-20

Season/Sunday: Any

Focus: Joshua was God's chosen leader after Moses. This sermon looks at Joshua's great courage, obedience, and faith as he led the Israelites to victory in Jericho.

Experience: The children will experience the story of the fall of Jericho by acting out the march around the wall of Jericho.

Arrangements: You will need seven trumpet-like instruments. Any noisemaker like whistles, toy flutes, and party blowers will suffice. You will also need some blocks to build a small wall (below waist-level). The cardboard kind of blocks or a dozen empty shoeboxes would be great! Note: This enactment, as presented, follows Scripture exactly. If you have limited time, you can eliminate the assignment of the priests and the sleeping/waking actions. Simply march around the walls six times for each day and do a day countdown. Then on the seventh day, do the countdown to seven.

> **Leader:** Good morning! (*As you talk, build the wall in the center of the space you will use to march.*) Today we're going to hear the story of a place called Jericho and a great leader called Joshua. This story happened a long, long time ago—before you, your mother, your grandfather, and your great-great-great-great-grandmother were born!
> Jericho had a strong, tall wall that went all the way around the city, protecting the people who lived inside. The people of Jericho were afraid of Joshua and his people called the Israelites, and so they hid behind their wall. Now—tell me, don't show me!—if you were Joshua and the Israelites, how would you make the wall fall down?

C: Knock it over. Stomp on it. Blow it up.

L: Those are all pretty good ideas, but God had a differ-ent idea. God said, "Joshua, I have delivered the land of Jericho into your hands. Now go and march around the city once with your army. Do this for six days and while you march have seven priests carry trumpets of rams' horns out in front. On the seventh day, march around the city seven times, with the priests blowing the trumpets. When they make the long blast, then have all the people give a loud shout, and then the wall of Jericho will fall down." Does that sound silly to you? Do you think walking around the wall several times will make the wall tumble down?

C: Yes. No.

L: Well, Joshua and the people probably did not think it was silly at all. They were very faithful and obedient people. They trusted God's word and did what God said. And we're going to do it too! Let's stand up and pretend to be them. Who wants to be Joshua?

C: (*Choose a child.*)

L: It's your job to count! And who wants to be the priests that sound the trumpets?

C: (*Choose the children and give them the noisemakers. If you have few children, let all of them be the priests and invite some nearby adults to be the rest of the army.*)

L: Now the rest of us will be the army. And when Joshua gives us the signal we have to give a loud shout. Are you all ready?
OK, now remember what God said to Joshua. We march around the wall once each day for six days. While we do that, priests, blow your horns! Let's march. (*Everybody marches around the wall once and the priests are using their noisemakers. Once the leader reaches the starting point again . . .*) Day one! Let's go to sleep. (*Put your hands together, place your hands next to your cheek and tilt your head to act out sleeping for a second.*) OK, wake up, next day. (*Stretch your arms and yawn.*) Let's march. (*Every-*

body *marches around the wall once, and the priests are using their noisemakers. Once the leader reaches the starting point again . . .*) Day two! (*Repeat the cycle until you reach day six. Once you get to day four, you may want to say, "This is hard work! And it requires a lot of patience!"*) OK, day six! Oh, tomorrow will be exciting. Let's go to sleep (*act out sleeping*).

OK, rise and shine, (*stretch*) it's the seventh day. Remember God said on the seventh day, we march around the city seven times. Joshua and everybody out there (*pointing to the pews*), you have to remember to count seven times. Because on the seventh time, Joshua, you will raise your hand up, the priests will give one last long trumpet sound, and the rest of you will then give a loud shout! Let's go!

C: (*Walk around the wall seven times. Remind Joshua to raise his hand, signal the priests to make one last sound, and get the army to shout. Then tip over the wall in the center to make it fall.*)

L: And just like God said, the wall of Jericho came tumbling down! You all did such a wonderful job! You were just like Joshua and the Israelites, faithful and obedient. Let's hold hands and ask God to help us be faithful and obedient every day . . . (*prayer*).

—*Joyce S. Fong*

Are You Happy?

Scripture: Psalm 119:1-3

Season/Sunday: Any

Focus: The One Hundred Ninteenth psalm is a poem in praise of God's word. In fact, every single one of its 176 verses (the longest chapter in the Bible!) makes mention of God's word in some way or another (decrees, precepts, ordinances, etc.). The focus of this sermon is how the Word celebrated in this psalm can make us happy.

Experience: The children will interact with a physical Bible in a variety of ways and also memorize a brief Bible verse.

Arrangements: None are needed, although the sermon assumes that there are Bibles to be found in the seats of the church (either in the pews or among the worshipers). Be sure to read the verses from the New Revised Standard or other some other version that translates the key word as "happy." Note that the movements of the sermon (seek, walk, keep) do not follow the order found in the verses.

Leader: Good morning! Let me read something from the Bible about being happy. (*Read Psalm 119:1-3.*) Did you hear how to be happy? It was right there in the words we just heard. It said happy are those who seek God and God's word with their whole heart. Hmmm, how could we <u>seek</u> God's word?

Children: Learn it, read it.

L: Those are great answers, but we have to find it, to seek it out, before we can learn it or read it. Let's go on a Word hunt right now—go out in the pews and see if you can find a Bible; hopefully it won't be too hard! Let's go and seek the Word of God.

C: (*Disperse to find Bibles. If most of the Bibles in your worship space are in the hands of those attending, you may want to encourage them to share.*)

L: Okay, now it also says in Psalm 119 that happy are those who <u>walk</u> in God's word. So, pick up your Bible and start walking back.

C: *(Return.)*

L: Of course, when the Bible says we are to walk in God's word, does it mean that we just carry around the Bible, just walk around with it?

C: Yes, no . . .

L: Well, the Bible is saying that we need to carry the Word of God in our heart—that way it can guide us. When we memorize God's Word, we're happy because it's there inside us no matter where we go. Hey, I know, let's memorize the next part! The Bible says, "Happy are those who keep God's word." Can you say that with me? Happy are those . . .

C: Happy are those . . .

L: . . . who keep . . .

C: . . . who keep . . .

L: . . . God's word.

C: . . . God's word.

L: Happy are those . . . who keep . . . God's word.

C: Happy are those . . . who keep . . . God's word.

L: Wow, that was great! And to help us remember that, let's hug God's word to our hearts, like we're really trying to keep it in there; and let's say our memory verse again.

L/C: *(while hugging Bible)* Happy are those . . . who keep . . . God's word.

L: That was great. Let's have a prayer and thank God for God's good word to us that can make us so happy . . . *(prayer). (After prayer)* Say, you know what, these verses also say, "Happy are those whose way is blameless." To be blameless means to be honest and right, and so let's be happy and honest by returning all these Bibles to where we got them! And as you do, why don't you say to the people nearby, "Be happy!"

C: *(Return Bibles as they return to seats.)*

—*Brant D. Baker*

I Found You!

Scripture: Luke 15:8-10

Season/Sunday: Any

Focus: The children will experience the great joy of finding something that is lost or being found when one is lost.

Experience: The leader will show ten coins (or other collectable) to talk about and then discover that one is missing. After a frantic search, with the children helping, everyone will experience great joy when the item is found.

Arrangements: This sermon uses ten different coins but can work with other collectibles, like stamps, rocks, pens, pins, and so forth. You will need a special box or bag to hold these items, and a cloth to clean them. Make sure you place nine of the items in the box and hide one in your Bible at Luke 15:8-10.

Leader:	Good morning, children! I am so excited because I have these special coins I want to show you. (*Change language throughout to reflect the collectable you have.*) I have exactly ten coins in this box, and I'm going to show them to you; but you have to promise to be careful. Do you promise to be careful?
Children:	Yes!
L:	Good (*opening box and taking out the coins one by one, giving each a quick polish and then laying them out in front of the children, continuing monologue*). Oh, they are so beautiful. I love these coins. I've traveled to a lot of places and each place I visit, I collect their coins. I keep them in this special box so that they are safe and I won't lose any of them. And I never lose anything, especially these coins. Nope, never! (*As you lay down the last one, show a worried look on your face.*) Wait a second! (*Point to each*

28

coin and count the coins.) One, two, three, four, five, six, seven, eight, nine. No, no, no, that can't be right. Help me count again.

C: One, two, three, four, five, six, seven, eight, nine.

L: Oh no! There are only nine coins! Where's my other coin? Did any of you see my tenth coin?

C: No. There are only nine. Is it in the box?

L: No, it's not in the box. (*Look at the people sitting in the pews.*) Did any of you see my tenth coin?

Congregation: No!

L: (*Looking more worried and agitated.*) Oh no, this is horrible. Where can it be? (*Start to frantically look for the coin: look in coin box again, stand up and check your pockets, and then start to crawl along, inviting the children and congregation to help.*) Can you please help me find the coin? See if you're sitting on my coin. Check your pockets. Check behind your ears. Check in front of you. Check behind you.

C: (*Start looking for the coin.*)

L: (*After about another minute of searching, flip through your Bible and find the coin. Leave the Bible open to that page—Luke 15:8-10.*) Ah! I found it! I found it! (*Dramatically overjoyed*) I found my coin! Oh, I'm so happy! Oh, thank you so much for helping me look for the coin! I found it. I found my coin. I must have left the coin in my Bible when I was preparing for the children's sermon this morning. Let me see what story I was going to tell you. Oh yes, that's funny. I was going to tell you a story Jesus told in Luke 15:8-10 about a woman who had . . . ten coins. Jesus said that if she lost one, she would light a lamp, sweep the house, and search carefully until she had found it. And when she found it, she would call together "her friends and neighbors, saying, 'Rejoice with me, for I have found the coin that I had lost.' Just so, I tell you, there is joy in the presence of the angels of God over one sinner who repents." Hmm . . . I wonder what that means. Do you know?

C: (*Offer some ideas.*)

29

L: Oh, I get it! Jesus seems to be saying that if any of us were ever lost, God would be very worried and sad and would look everywhere for us too. And when God finds us, there will be a pretty big party in heaven! Let's have a prayer and give thanks that we're so important to God . . . *(prayer)*.

—*Joyce S. Fong*

Becoming a Child of God

Scripture: 1 John 3:1

Season/Sunday: Lent

Focus: To learn our identity as children of God.

Experience: To experience how we become children of God. When God wanted to tell us how much we are loved, God did not send a memo, he sent a person, Jesus Christ. In like manner God sends other people to show us we are precious and loved by God. We become children of God by being loved.

Arrangements: None are needed; however, if your congregation is not used to participating in children's sermons, you may want to prepare one or two people ahead of time to come forward on your cue and be prepared to give the children a hug and tell them they are special children of God.

Leader: Good morning, boys and girls. Let me ask you something this morning. Who are you?

Children: I'm Jamie. I'm Brian. I'm Natash.

L: That's right! Those are your names. Do you know who else you are?

C: My mommy's daughter?

L: That's right too! How about this: how many of you are also a child of God?

C: Me! Me too!

L: That's right! We are all children of God. But how do you know you are a child of God?

C: You told me I was. The Bible tells me so.

L: Those are good answers! When God wanted us to know that we are really God's children, God gave us the Bible; but what else did God do?

C: (*May or may not have any more ideas.*)

L: When God wanted us to know, really know deep down that we are loved and we are God's children,

31

God sent a person to tell us that. God sent his only Son, Jesus Christ. But even then, God wasn't done. (*Looking at the adults*) God wants our children to know, really know that they are children of God, that God loves them. Another way God has to tell them that is through us. We need some people to come and give them this message. (*Counting kids*) we need fourteen people or more to come forward, give each one of these kids a hug, and say they are God's special children. (*Encourage adults to come forward. After they have interacted with children and returned to their seats, address the children again.*) So, let me ask you one more time; who are you?

C: Children of God!

L: That's right! Let's have a prayer and thank God that we are, and ask God to help us tell some other people that good news as well . . . (*prayer*).

—*Jeff Hutcheson*

Seeing the Sin

Scripture: Psalm 51:1-12

Season/Sunday: Lent (or with a baptism)

Focus: Although we are all sinners and can see our sin, in mercy and grace God wipes away our sin and sees us as forgiven.

Experience: The children will see their faces marked by sin and will see that God has wiped away their sin and sees them as a forgiven sinner.

Arrangements: A large mirror, a washable marker, window cleaner with a label "GRACE," and paper towels. Keep the window cleaner and paper towels hidden until later in the message.

Leader: Good morning to you all! Today we are going to talk about a church word, "sin." Can you tell me some things that we might call sins?

Children: Not listening to your parents. Stealing. Hitting.

L: Wow, that's a lot of things. Let's write down some of them (*use the marker to write some of the sins on the mirror making the words large enough to block a clear view on the mirror*). That's a great list . . . sounds like you know what sin is. Sin is anything that hurts our friendship with God or with other people. For example, if we don't listen to our parents, they get mad or maybe we get hurt. God says it is wrong to steal and if we steal something from somebody, it hurts our friendship with them.
Now if I turn this mirror around to you, what do you see?

C: We can't see—all the words are in the way. It's like it's written all over our face.

L: That's right! You see your face, but you also see the sins. That's what the person who wrote Psalm 51 saw. He said we can see all the things we do wrong,

33

and he asks God to take away the sin. What can take away these sins?

C: Ask forgiveness. Say we're sorry.

L: The Bible tells us to ask God: "Have mercy on me, O God, because of your unfailing love. Because of your great care, take away the stain of my sins. Wash me clean from my guilt. Clean me from my sin" (from Psalm 51:1-2). The person who wrote these words knew that only by God's mercy, or grace, could we become clean again. So let's try that. (*Bring out the window cleaner with the label "GRACE." Spray the mirror and wipe it clean with the paper towels.*) Now what do you see?

C: (*Looking in the clean mirror*) I see me!

L: Do you still see any of that sin?

C: No!

L: Well, neither does God! Through Jesus and his death on the cross, God has forgiven our sins and has made us clean. Now when God looks at us, there isn't any sin but only the faces of God's children! That forgiveness is a gift from God. Isn't that wonderful?!
During Lent we spend time thinking about how Jesus came to make us clean from our sins . . . OR
In baptism we celebrate being made clean from our sins and being God's child.
And we can do that same thing for other people. When people do something wrong, we can forgive them just as God forgives us. Let's have a prayer and thank God for this wonderful gift we've been given, and that we can pass it on to others . . . *(prayer)*.

—*Paula Hoffman*

Hosanna!

Scripture: Mark 11:1-11

Season/Sunday: Palm Sunday

Focus: The children will learn that Palm Sunday was a day of celebration for some of the people of Jerusalem who looked forward to Jesus' arrival. The children will learn that in those times people used palm leaves to celebrate, and that the cry for joy, "Hosanna," means "Save" or "We pray."

Experience: The children will reenact the triumphal entry of Jesus into Jerusalem.

Arrangements: Collect various items used for celebrations such as balloons, noisemakers, streamers, rose petals, signs, flags, tambourines, and so forth. There is no limit to how many you can use, but no need to use more than two or three. You will need a few large palm leaves and a few pieces of cloth (or some actual cloaks). Ask some adult helpers to help manage the distribution of these items and to guide the reenactment, and arrange for one adult to be Jesus.

> **Leader:** Good morning! (*Setting out or uncovering all of the celebration materials where the children can see them*) Wow, what all do I have here?
>
> **Children:** (*Identify celebration items*)
>
> **L:** What are all these things used for?
>
> **C:** Parties!
>
> **L:** That's right; but let's be specific, what kind of parties or celebrations?
>
> **C:** Birthday parties. Weddings. New Years. Weddings. Graduations.
>
> **L:** Okay, but what about these (*show palms and cloaks*)? What kind of celebration would we use these for?
>
> **C:** (*May or may not know*)
>
> **L:** Well, back a long time ago in the time of Jesus people used palm branches and cloaks as part of a celebration

we call Palm Sunday. It was such a big party we can find the story in all four gospels in the New Testament—Matthew, Mark, Luke, and John. Here's what happened: Because of the many things he had done and said, Jesus had become very famous. Many people knew about him, and wherever he went they gathered to see him. One day Jesus was going into Jerusalem. When the people found out he was coming, they got really excited and decided to celebrate. They wanted to throw Jesus the biggest welcome party ever!

Now here's the fun part! Let's all pretend to travel back in time to this celebration, except let's bring some of our own things to celebrate (*with adult helpers begin to distribute the celebration items*). Once you have something, let's go and stand along the sides of the aisles and get ready for Jesus' arrival.

C: (*Take items and move to aisle.*)

L: Now, there's one other thing you need to know. On that day, a long time ago, as Jesus arrived and the people celebrated, they shouted out, "Hosanna!" Do you know what *Hosanna* means?

C: Hallelujah? Praise?

L: It can mean those things, and it literally means "save us." Today we might yell out "Woo hoo!" or "Yeah!" and "Help us!" And while they shouted out their *hosannas,* they waved the palm branches and put their cloaks on the road to make a kind of red carpet for Jesus. So, are you ready? (*Cue for adult helper who is Jesus.*) Here comes Jesus, and so let the celebration start! Wave those palm branches and signs and flags, blow those noisemakers, throw those rose petals, and remember to shout out, "Hosanna!" And all of you (*indicating people in the pews*) can help too! Clap your hands, stomp your feet, and yell out, "Hosanna!"

(*After Jesus passes and celebration subsides*) that was wonderful! Let's have a prayer and thank God that we can celebrate Jesus today . . . (*prayer*).

—Joyce S. Fong

Sowing Imperishable Seed

Scripture: 1 Corinthians 15:35-44

Season/Sunday: Easter

Focus: Most children (and most adults) can grasp the image of the empty tomb. More challenging is to grasp what that empty tomb might mean. The early church saw the resurrection in terms of "new life," an image that takes root (!) in Paul's discussion of planting imperishable seed.

Experience: To see various seeds and what they become, and then to become a seed ourselves, growing into God.

Arrangements: You will need two or three different representations of seeds and what they become. In the sermon below there were (1) a grass seed and a piece or clump of grass, (2) a bulb (any kind) and an Easter lily, and (3) an egg and a baby chick (ambitious but well worth it!). If you do use a baby chick, it might be wise to have a helper keep it well hidden and out of the area until time.

Leader: Good morning, happy Easter, it's a beautiful day; and doesn't everybody just look so <u>alive</u>! Are you all feeling pretty alive today?

Children: Yes!

L: That's good. But it makes me wonder, where does life come from?

C: From God. From mommies and daddies.

L: Those are really good answers! Well, let me ask you this (*bringing out a grass seed*), what's this?

C: A seed?

L: That's right, it's a grass seed. Does life come from this?

C: Yes.

L: Yeah, somehow God gives life to the seed, and the seed gives life to this (*bringing out clump of grass*).

37

Okay, what about this? (*Show bulb, perhaps making a disgusted face.*)

C: Eeew. Another kind of seed?

L: That's right, it's called a "bulb," and it works a little differently than a seed. Can you believe that this ugly thing will someday give life to this beautiful thing (*indicate Easter lily*)? Here again, God gives life to the seed, and the seed gives life to something completely different, something much more beautiful than what you would think. Okay, what's this (*showing egg*)?

C: An egg!

L: That's right, and you may not know this, but an egg is another kind of seed. But does it get planted in the ground?

C: No!

L: No, but somehow God gives life to it, and we get what Grayden is bringing over to us (*helper brings baby chick*).

C: Ooh! (*Give children time to interact with chick.*)

L: The grass seed, the Easter lily bulb, and the egg are all seeds of some kind that God uses to give life, and in each case could you guess what the life would look like from looking at the seed?

C: No!

L: No, it's amazing, isn't it? Well, did you know that your body is a seed?

C: It is? No it's not!

L: Absolutely it is! In the Bible it says that when we die it's like planting a kind of seed, and that at the resurrection what is planted without honor will be raised in glory, what is planted in weakness will be raised in power, and what is planted as a physical body will be raised as a spiritual body (1 Corinthians 15: 42-44). What do you think?

C: Weird.

L: Yeah, I know, but pretty cool too, huh? Let's have a prayer and give thanks for the whole mysterious way that God brings life, new life, and new creation out of something that is dead . . . (*prayer*).

—*Brant D. Baker*

And God Saw That It Was Good!

Scripture: Excerpts from Genesis 1:1–2:3

Season/Sunday: Any, although the sermon would be particularly appropriate for an Earth Day celebration.

Focus: The sermon will help children identify that God is all around us, revealed in creation.

Experience: The children will appreciate and experience the creation story by using all their senses to act out the story.

Arrangements: You will need a Bible, a narrator, a copy of the script below, and the awareness of the wonderful creation around you! Be sure the narrator and the leader practice the script together at least once or twice. The timing is important. The leader will guide the children in doing all of the hand motions. You may choose to modify them; do whatever is natural to the leader and the children. Be "creative"!

> **Leader:** Good morning! This is the day that the Lord has made, and God saw that it was good! Today I have a glorious story to share with you. It is the very first story from the Bible, from the book of Genesis (*hold the Bible up for all the children to see and open to Genesis*). It is a story about God's creation. (*Narrator's name*) is going to read the story, and we're going to help! Let's listen and follow my motions:
>
> **Narrator:** "In the beginning when God created the heavens and the earth, the earth was a formless void and darkness covered the face of the deep, while a wind from God swept over the face of the waters."
>
> **Leader:** Let's wave our arms back and forth and blow like the wind. (*Leader and children do the motions.*)
>
> **Narrator:** "Then God said, 'Let there be light'; and there was light. And God saw that the light was good; and God separated the light from the darkness."

Leader: Ooh, that light is bright, let's put on our sunglasses. (*Leader and children pretend to put on their sunglasses.*)

Narrator: "God called the light Day, and the darkness he called Night. And there was evening and there was morning, the first day."

Leader: (*Hold up one finger for the first day. For each "evening" and "morning" throughout, Leader and children act as if going to sleep and then waking up.*)

Narrator: "And God said, 'Let there be a dome in the midst of the waters, and let it separate the waters from the waters.' So God made the dome and separated the waters that were under the dome from the waters that were above the dome. And it was so. God called the dome Sky."

Leader: Let's stretch out our hands and reach for the skies. (*Leader and children do the motions.*)

Narrator: "And there was evening and there was morning, the second day."

Leader: (*Hold up two fingers for the second day; do sleep and wake-up motion.*)

Narrator: "And God said, 'Let the waters under the sky be gathered together into one place, and let the dry land appear.' And it was so. God called the dry land Earth . . ."

Leader: (*Leader and children flatten hands and spread them as if flattening land.*)

Narrator: " . . . and the waters that were gathered together he called Seas."

Leader: (*Wave hands up and down.*)

All: **"And God saw that it was good."** (*From here on, say, "And God saw that it was good" with the narrator.*)

Narrator: "Then God said, 'Let the earth put forth vegetation: plants yielding seed, and fruit trees of every kind on earth that bear fruit with the seed in it.' And it was so. The earth brought forth vegetation: plants yielding seed of every kind, and trees of every kind bearing fruit with the seed in it."

Leader: Mmmm . . . let's grab some broccoli, carrots, and spinach. Let's pick some apples and oranges from these trees. (*Leader and children pretend to pick the vegetables and fruit.*)

All: **"And God saw that it was good."**

Narrator: "And there was evening and there was morning, the third day."

Leader: (*Hold up three fingers for the third day. Sleep/Wake motion.*)

Narrator: "And God said, 'Let there be lights in the dome of the sky to separate the day from the night; and let them be for signs and for seasons and for days and years, and let them be lights in the dome of the sky to give light upon the earth.' And it was so. . . . "

Leader: Who can show me the sun shining brightly? Good thing we have our sunglasses on!

All: **"And God saw that it was good."**

Narrator: "And there was evening and there was morning, the fourth day."

Leader: (*Hold up four fingers for day four. Sleep/Wake motion.*)

Narrator: "And God said, 'Let the waters bring forth swarms of living creatures, and let birds fly above the earth across the dome of the sky.'"

Leader: Let's flap our wings, fly, and look down on God's creation. (*Leader and children act it out.*)

Narrator: "So God created the great sea monsters and every living creature that moves, of every kind, with which the waters swarm, and every winged bird of every kind."

Leader: Let me see some sharks, dolphins, whales, frogs, and crabs. (*Leader and children act it out.*)

All: **"And God saw that it was good."**

Narrator: "God blessed them, saying, 'Be fruitful and multiply and fill the waters in the seas, and let birds multiply on the earth.' And there was evening and there was morning, the fifth day."

Leader: (*Hold up five fingers for day five. Sleep/Wake motion.*)

Narrator: "And God said, 'Let the earth bring forth living creatures of every kind: cattle and creeping things and wild animals of the earth of every kind.' And it was so. God made the wild animals of the earth of every kind, and the cattle of every kind, and everything that creeps upon the ground of every kind."

Leader: Let me see all the different land animals, like tigers, giraffes, lions, bear, squirrels, cows and pigs. (*Leader and children act it out.*)

All: **"And God saw that it was good."**

Narrator: "Then God said, 'Let us make humankind in our image, according to our likeness; and let them have dominion over the fish of the sea, and over the birds of the air, and over the cattle, and over all the wild animals of the earth, and over every creeping thing that creeps upon the earth.' So God created humankind in his image, in the image of God he created them; male and female he created them. God blessed them . . . "

Leader: (*While the narrator is saying the previous lines, point to yourself and one another for humankind.*)

All: "And God saw that it was good."

Narrator: "And there was evening and there was morning, the sixth day."

Leader: (*Hold up six fingers for day six. Sleep/Wake motion.*)

Narrator: "Thus the heavens and the earth were finished, and all their multitude. And on the seventh day God finished the work that he had done, and he rested on the seventh day from all the work that he had done. So God blessed the seventh day and hallowed it, because on it God rested from all the work that he had done in creation."

Leader: (*Fold arms on chest and appear satisfied with a big sigh, sit down and rest!*)

Leader: Isn't the story of creation wonderful? I hope you enjoyed it as much as I did! It reminds us of how everything was made, and that God is all around us. Let's have a prayer and give thanks for all creation, asking God to help us take care of it . . . (*prayer*).

—*Joyce S. Fong*

Feed My Lambs

Scripture: John 21:1-17

Season/Sunday: Second or third Sunday after Easter. Also appropriate for a food drive mission (*see alternative ending at the end of the sermon*). Note: this alternative requires a two-week lead-in to announce the food drive, but is worth it to help drive home the point of "feeding" Christ's sheep.

Focus: On the third appearance to the disciples after resurrection Jesus commanded Peter to feed his lambs. This sermon focuses on how we can all take care of one another.

Experience: The children will form a loose circle (*or several concentric circles if there are a lot of children*). Each time Jesus asks Peter whether he loves him, Peter responds with a yes and Jesus commands Peter to feed his lambs, the children will step forward making the circle tighter. By the third time, the children will have their arms around each other.

Arrangements: Think through where you will have enough space to carry out the experience described above. You may need to go to the narthex (entry space). If you have a lot of children, several adult helpers may be beneficial. Note alternative ending below that uses a pre-announced food drive.

Leader: Good morning! A few Sundays ago [*or last Sunday*] we celebrated Jesus rising from the dead. After Jesus rose from the dead, he appeared to the disciples several times on earth. The story about the third time he appeared is in John 21. (*Optional: open the Bible to John 21.*) On that day Simon Peter and some of the other disciples were fishing. They had been fishing all night but had caught nothing. Just after daybreak, a stranger stood on the beach and called to them, "Do you have any fish for me to eat?" They answered him, "No." Then, this stranger said to them, "Cast

43

the net to the right side of the boat, and you will find some." So the disciples did that, and all of a sudden, their nets were full of fish. Then, they remembered how a long time ago, someone had done the same thing with them. Who do you think this stranger is?

Children: Another disciple? Jesus?

L: You're right! The disciples suddenly recognized Jesus and said, "It is the Lord!" So they came ashore, took some of the fish, and had breakfast together.
Now before I finish the story, I need your help with the ending. Let's all stand and form a circle. (*The children and helpers stand up and form one or several loose concentric layered circles depending on the size of the group. Make sure there is space between the children.*) OK, now we're ready. After Jesus and the disciples were finished with breakfast, Jesus said to Simon Peter, "Simon son of John, do you love me more than these?" Simon Peter said, "Yes, Lord, I love you." Can we all say that? Say, "Yes, Lord . . . "

C: Yes, Lord . . .

L: " . . . I love you."

C: I love you.

L: Jesus said to him, "Feed my lambs." Children, let's all take one step forward toward the center of the circle.

C: (*Move. Each child should be standing closer to a neighbor. The circle(s) should be tighter.*)

L: A second time Jesus said to Simon Peter, "Simon son of John, do you love me?" Peter said (*prompt children*),

C: Yes, Lord, I love you.

L: Jesus said, "Tend my sheep." And let's all take another step forward toward the center of the circle and hold hands with the person next to you.

C: (*Take step and hold hands.*)

L: Jesus said to Simon Peter the third time, "Simon son of John, do you love me?" (*Cue children to reply.*)

C: Yes, Lord, I love you.

L: But this time Simon Peter felt hurt because Jesus had asked him three times. And again Jesus said to him, "Feed my sheep." And so let's take one more step forward toward the center of the circle and put our arms around each other.

C: (*Children make last step forward and place arms around person next to them. The circle(s) should be tight.*)

L: Who are the lambs that Jesus commands us to love?

C: Peter? The disciples? One another?

L: That's right, Jesus' lambs are all those who love Jesus: the people next to you, in front of you, in back of you, sitting in the pews, and all around you. Let's have a prayer and ask God to help us care for one another in this special way . . . *(prayer)*.

Alternative Addition: A food drive can be incorporated into this sermon. Arrange a week or two beforehand for children to bring a can to contribute to the food drive during the children's sermon time. Instead of forming the circle immediately for the ending of the story (*for example, the Jesus question, Simon Peter response, and Jesus command cycle*), divide the children into three groups. On the first Jesus command, "Feed my lambs," have the first group of children bring their canned food to the center and start forming a circle. On the second command, have the second group of children do the same thing and join the circle or form a second circle around the first. On the third command, the last group of children will bring their canned food to the center and complete the circle. This activity makes the passage life-connecting and meaningful.

—*Joyce S. Fong*

The Good Shepherd

Scripture: John 10:1-10

Season/Sunday: Any

Focus: Jesus is the good shepherd who cares for us and watches over us. Jesus calls out to each of us by name. We should grow to learn to recognize the voice of Jesus so that we can follow the good shepherd.

Experience: The children will experience the scripture passage through the game "Simon says/Jesus Says."

Arrangements: You will need one adult helper who acts out as "the stranger" and interrupts the leader to make the sheep stray. The helper should sit with the children and be part of the group from the beginning of the sermon. Although not an absolute requirement, the sermon assumes that the "Good Shepherd" leader knows the name of each of the "sheep." If, as the leader, you don't know each child by name, it might be helpful to have nametags prepared in advance (*have a few blank extras with a marker for any unexpected children*). Ask an adult helper to aid in the distribution of the nametags to help move things along.

> **Leader:** Good morning! Let's start off by playing a game of "Simon Says." Remember that you only do the things that Simon says to do. If you do not hear "Simon says," then you don't do it. Let's start this game. Simon says stand up!
>
> **Children:** (*Children stand up, along with leader and helper.*)
>
> **L:** Simon says touch your head.
>
> **C:** (*All touch their heads.*)
>
> **L:** Simon says touch your nose.
>
> **C:** (*All touch their noses.*)
>
> **L:** Simon says touch your toes.
>
> **C:** (*All touch their toes.*)
>
> **Helper:** (*Jumping to the center and interrupting*) Simon says

46

jump around! (*Helper and maybe some children jump around.*)

L: Wait a second. I'm the leader. I'm the only one who can say "Simon says"! Don't follow the wrong Simon! (*Helper rejoins the group.*) Simon says hop on one foot.

C: (*All hop on one foot.*)

L: Simon says make a silly face.

C: (*All make a silly face.*)

Helper: (*Again jumping to the center and interrupting*) Simon says clap your hands. (*Helper and maybe some children clap their hands.*)

L: (*Dramatically scanning the area for children who are clapping their hands.*) Ooh, I hope no one followed the wrong leader. (*Helper rejoins the group.*) All right, Simon says, everyone sit down quietly on that side (*leader points to one side of the area*) and get your listening ears ready. (*Everyone sits down on the assigned side. The leader stands on the opposite side.*) There is a story in the Gospel of John. One day, Jesus was teaching lots of people a lesson about who he was. Jesus said, "There is a good shepherd, someone who watches over and takes care of his sheep. The good shepherd knows each of his sheep by name, and his sheep recognize his voice. So each time the shepherd calls, the sheep will follow him. But if a stranger calls them, the sheep will not listen and will run away." Now let's play a game like "Simon Says," but instead I will say, "The Good Shepherd says." Remember only do what the good shepherd says. The good shepherd says, *child1 name, child2 name,* and *child3 name,* come over here and sit with me (*if possible, call each child by his or her name throughout*).

C: (*The called children walk over and sit on the side where the leader is sitting.*)

L: The good shepherd says, *child4 name, child5 name,* and *child6 name,* come over here and sit with me.

C: (*The called children walk over and sit on the side where the leader is sitting. Continue until about half of the children are called.*)

Helper: (*Jumping up*) *child6 name, child7 name,* and *child8 name,* come over here and sit with me!

   L: You're not the good shepherd. They will not listen to you! They will not follow you! (*Helper sits back down.*) The good shepherd says, (*call all remaining children*) come over here and sit with me.

   C: (*The called children walk over and sit on the side where the leader is sitting.*)

   L: Now that we have all our sheep sitting together with the good shepherd, let me finish the story. While Jesus was telling the people this story, the people were very confused. They wondered what this had to do with Jesus. Then Jesus explained, "I am the good shepherd, and you are my sheep. I will always care for you. Therefore, you must know my voice and follow me."

Let's have a prayer and thank God that every day when we read the Bible, pray, sing praises, and talk to our family and friends about Jesus, we learn more about Jesus and grow to recognize his voice . . . (*prayer*).

Alternate ending: Let's practice that now. Jesus says, let's all shake hands and be friends. (*All shake one another's hands.*) Jesus says, let's all hug each other and show our love for each other. (*All hug one another.*) Jesus says, let's hold hands and pray . . . (*prayer*).

—*Joyce S. Fong*

Pneumanauts

Scripture: John 3:8

Season/Sunday: Pentecost

Focus: To learn a new word for spirit (*pneuma*) and a new way of thinking about being a disciple ("Pneumanaut"—a term originally coined by Len Sweet).

Experience: To learn fun new words and ways to say them.

Arrangements: None are needed.

Leader:	Good morning, everyone. How are you today?
Children:	Good!
L:	Do you know what you want to be when you grow up?
C:	A cook. A doctor.
L:	That's great. Do you know what I wanted to be when I grew up?
C:	A preacher?
L:	Nope. At least for a little while I wanted to be an astronaut *(or, "Do any of you think you'd want to be an astronaut?")* You know, one of those people who ride on a space ship into outer space.
C:	Cool. I want to be an astronaut too.
L:	I even had a toy space capsule with a space man inside. With my imagination I could blast him off into orbit, and then open the doors and send him on a space walk.
C:	I have a Buzz Lightyear toy!
L:	That's fun! Well, anyway, I never became an astronaut. I never blasted off into outer space. But you know what? I become another kind of explorer. I became a Pneumanaut.
C:	A what?
L:	A Pneumanaut. Try to say it with me . . . *(pronounce it slowly)* <u>Pneu</u>-ma-naut.

C: Pneu-ma-naut.

L: That's great! The word *Pneumanaut* comes from two other words. The first is the Greek word *pneuma,* which means *wind* or *spirit.* Can you say *pneuma?*

C: *Pneuma.*

L: Since it's a word that can mean wind, maybe we should say it in a windy way, *Pneuuuuuu-maaa* (*say it with a lot of exaggerated breath*).

C: *Pneuuuuuu-maaaa.*

L: Oh, that was good! The other part of *Pneumanaut* comes from the Greek word *nautes,* which means sailor. So, that would mean a Pneumanaut is a wind sailor. But this isn't wind surfing! It's much more exciting than that! A Pneumanaut is someone who sails on the winds of God's Spirit. Let's all stand up and pretend! (*Encourage everyone to strike a surfer pose and pretend to try and keep balance as you weave back and forth. The congregation could be encouraged here to make wind sounds as background for the rest of the sermon.*) That's what a disciple of Jesus is supposed to do. Are you a disciple of Jesus?

C: (*As they "surf" along*) Yes!

L: Good! All of us disciples are actually Pneumanauts because we sail on the Spirit of God. And the church holiday we are celebrating today—Pentecost—is the time we talk about God giving that gift of Spirit. It was on Pentecost, more than two thousand years ago, that God gave the *pneuma,* the Spirit, to the first disciples. And since we are also disciples, we want to learn how to let God's windy Spirit take us on the journey of a lifetime! We're all Pneumanauts!

C: I still want to be a cook when I grow up.

L: You can still be a cook . . . on the Pneumanaut ship! Let's pray and thank God for the exciting trip ahead . . . *(prayer).*

—*Jeff Hutcheson*

Clothe Yourselves with Splendor

Scripture: Psalm 45:2 (NIV)

Season/Sunday: Mother's Day, but note that this sermon could stand alone or as part of a series entitled "Dressing Up for God."

Focus: Dressing our best for God.

Experience: Answering the question of why we have to get "scrubbed-up" and "dressed-up" for church.

Arrangements: None, but think through the customs of your particular church, including possible differences between contemporary and traditional worship, and how you will speak about the issue of "looking our best" for God.

Leader: Good morning, children. What day is today?
Children: Mother's Day!
L: That's right! So, what did you do to get ready for church today? Did you go outside and get all dirty and put on your very worst clothes to come to church?
C: No! We made Mommy breakfast in bed.
L: That was a nice thing to do. And after that, you got dressed for church, didn't you? Did you wear your pajamas to church?
C: No! We had to put on "church" clothes.
L: That's right. What kind of clothes do you wear to church?
C: Nice ones. Our best ones. My mommy doesn't let me wear jeans.
L: You know, boys and girls, not everyone around the world has nice clothes or nice mommies either; but this is a day when we try to look our best and honor our mommies. So we all scrubbed and cleaned, and then put on something clean and nice to come to church. And, since its Mother's Day, you might even

have put on something that your mom wanted you to wear even if you didn't want to wear it.

Well, did you know that God likes it when you look your very best? God says in the Bible in Psalm 45, "clothe yourself with splendor." That means not only wearing our nice clothes as a sign of respect for our mothers or even for God, but it also means putting on our nice manners too!

So, everyone stand up! And let's pretend we're putting on different pieces of clothing, but instead of calling them pants and shirts and shoes, let's call them different manners. What's an important manner we should put on every day?

C: Politeness. Respectfulness. Niceness.

L: Wow, that's great. Let's first pretend we're putting on the shirt of politeness.

C: *(All pretend.)*

L: And now let's pretend to put on the pants of respect.

C: *(All pretend.)*

L: And what else? Oh yes, niceness. What piece of clothing should that be?

C: Shoes. Belt. Jacket.

L: Well, put on whichever one of those you think you need most. For me, it's the belt of niceness. That's all part of the splendor we should put on every day, and there's probably even more pieces of splendorous clothing we can think of on our own later today! Let's have a prayer and thank God that when we clothe ourselves with splendor, it helps us honor those around us and feel better inside and out . . . *(prayer)*.

—*Bob Sharman*

Clothe Yourselves with Humility

Scripture: 1 Peter 5:5 (NIV)

Season/Sunday: Any, but note that this sermon could stand alone or as part of a series entitled "Dressing Up for God."

Focus: This sermon attempts to get at the challenging notion of how we can "clothe" ourselves with humility.

Experience: Enacting Peter's words, first the wrong way, followed by a much better way.

Arrangements: Leader will need to bring a bag full of old torn-up adult-sized clothing, and a Bible.

Leader: Good morning, everyone! Listen to what Peter says to us in 1 Peter 5:5 (*reading from Bible*) "all of you, clothe yourselves with humility." Did you hear that? Clothe yourselves with humility all of you. Let's do that! I brought some clothes today, and these clothes will help us feel very humble, don't you think? (*Pass out shirts, sweaters, pants to various children.*) Put these on, and I think you will feel humble. Here's one for you. I think I'm gonna put this one on (*leader puts on a piece of clothing*).

Children: (*Giggles.*)

L: Wait a minute: why aren't you putting on the clothes? Don't you want to clothe yourselves with humility like Peter says?

C: No!

L: Well, how do you think we can do what Peter asks? Is there something we can do to be humble? What do you think?

C: We could throw these clothes away!

L: Well, they are very old clothes, you're right. But what does it mean to be humble?

C: (*May or may not have any ideas.*)

L: Humility has to do with not being selfish, with not demanding our own way. Humility is thinking of others before thinking of ourselves, or putting other people and their needs ahead of our own. What could we do as Christians to think of others even before we think about ourselves?

C: Pray for them? Help them?

L: I think you are exactly right. Who is someone we could pray for? (*At this point the leader may wish to prompt a particular mission or service connection; or brothers and sisters or preschool and school mates.*) Okay, let's humbly pray for them right now . . . (*prayer*).

—*Bob Sharman*

Clothe Yourselves with Strength

Scripture: Isaiah 52:1 (NIV)

Season/Sunday: Any, but note that this sermon could stand alone or as part of a series entitled "Dressing Up for God."

Focus: How we "put on" strength by memorizing God's word.

Experience: Remembering scripture in order to become spiritually strong.

Arrangements: A large Bible, perhaps even one of the pulpit-sized Bibles.

Leader: Good morning, everyone. Listen to what a fellow in the Bible named Isaiah says: "Awake, awake . . . clothe yourself with strength" (NIV).
We know that to clothe ourselves means to put on our clothes, like our pants or dresses or shirts. But Isaiah is saying we should clothe ourselves with something else too. What is it that Isaiah tells us we should clothe ourselves with when we wake up each day?

Children: Our school clothes. Our church clothes. Strength.

L: Yes, did someone say "strength"? That's right. But how do we clothe ourselves with strength?

C: You pick up heavy things!

L: That's true, picking up heavy things will make us strong. But what could Isaiah mean when he says, "clothe yourself with strength"?

C: One time my daddy picked up me and my sister!

L: Wow, that takes strength! Do you think you could get strong picking up this big Bible? Who wants to try?

C: (*Take turns lifting—Leader could take on the role of a weight trainer, encouraging, counting number of reps, and so forth.*)

L: You know, somehow this doesn't seem quite right. Is this what Isaiah means when he tells us to clothe ourselves with strength?

C: No!

L: No, he means to become strong in the Lord. He means become strong on the inside. One way to become strong on the inside is to learn what God says in the Bible. We don't need to lift this Bible; we need to look inside of it, and that will help us become strong on the inside of us.

So let's memorize a verse today; and tonight before you go to bed and tomorrow when you wake up, be sure to say this verse. Then you will be strong for the day—on the inside! (*Here leader may use any appropriate verse to teach the children, for example the first part of John 3:16 or John 14:6, or an appropriate phrase or verse from the text used for the other sermon of the day. Use an echo-response method of teaching, asking that the children remember increasingly longer sections of the verse. Be sure to repeat it enough that there's a good chance they will remember!*)

That was great! Let's have a prayer and give thanks that God has provided this way for us to put on strength . . . (*prayer*).

—*Bob Sharman*

Clothe Yourselves with Jesus

Scripture: Romans 13:14 (NIV)

Season/Sunday: Any, but note that this sermon could stand alone or as part of a series entitled "Dressing Up for God." This sermon would also be excellent for use in conjunction with a baptism.

Focus: How in the world can we follow Paul's advice to clothe ourselves with Jesus?

Experience: Receiving the cross of Jesus as part of the baptismal "clothes" in which we live as Christians.

Arrangements: A small amount of water needs to be put in the baptismal font. If a font is not part of your tradition, or if the font is not convenient to the area for the children's sermon, a small bowl filled with water will do.

Leader: Hello, everyone! Gather in closely because I'm having some trouble with something. You know, we've been talking about different kinds of clothes in the Bible. But you'll never guess what Paul says this time about clothes in Romans 13:14, "Clothe yourselves with the <u>Lord Jesus Christ</u>. . . . " What does Paul mean? How can we clothe ourselves with Jesus Christ?

Children: Put on Jesus? Make a Jesus shirt? You have Jesus in your heart.

L: That's right. And that is very important. Also, it's good to keep God's word from the Bible in our hearts. But how can we <u>clothe</u> ourselves with Jesus; how can we put on Christ?

C: (*Blank looks—must be a sleepy Sunday!*)

L: Well, I've been thinking hard about this, and I had an idea. Christians forever have used the mark of the cross on their forehead to remember that they live under the cross of Jesus, like the mark some people get with ashes on Ash Wednesday. The cross on our foreheads is a kind of clothes of Jesus. Do you suppose we could put on that clothing of Jesus right now?

C: Yes!

L: And today, instead of ashes, we'll use water from the baptismal font. This isn't a baptism, that's a different way we put on Jesus; but it can remind us of baptism and help us to remember it. Come here around the font, and let me put on the clothing-cross of Jesus!

C: (*Receive this mark. Leader may want to say, "Remember your baptism and be thankful" or "Clothe yourself with the Lord Jesus Christ" or some other appropriate phrase.*)

L: Okay, how did that feel?

C: Good. Wet.

L: (*Laughs*) Let's have a prayer and ask Jesus to help us remember to put him on every day . . . *(prayer).*

—*Bob Sharman*

A Heavenly Hug

Scripture: Revelation 21:1-4

Season/Sunday: Father's Day

Focus: Heaven can be hard to imagine. Is it going to be a holy place where we only do holy-sounding things, or will there be more basic human delights? By linking this topic to Father's Day, this sermon is focused on the familial aspects of our heavenly home.

Experience: This sermon engages the children's imagination in wondering what heaven might be like. Have fun with this!

Arrangements: None are necessary, but since not all children present will have a father with them, the sermon calls for children to bring their entire family forward.

> **Leader:** Good morning! I'd like to invite the children to come forward and bring their entire family with them. That's rights, moms, dads, brothers and sisters, grandparents . . . anyone you've got with you today, bring 'em down. Great to see you all. I have a question for the children: what is heaven going to be like?
>
> **Children:** Pretty. Golden. Boring.
>
> **L:** Boring?! Oh, not for me! I'm planning on worshiping God for, oh, I don't know, 10,000 years or so, and then I'm going to take a few days and play golf. What about you? What do you think heaven will be like; what will you do there?
>
> **Child:** Play with my friends?
>
> **L:** That sounds good. Anyone else with an idea . . . what will you do in heaven?
>
> **C:** Pray. Sing. Go fishing.
>
> **L:** Those sound like good things too! We can't know for sure what heaven will be like. The Bible says that it will be all new, and that God will be with us, and

beyond that, it's hard to imagine. But let me ask you this, does God love us?

C: Yes!

L: That's right, and because God loves us, we know God wants the best for us. Has God given us a lot of good things to enjoy here on earth?

C: Yes!

L: That's right, and if God has given us so much good here on earth, we can only believe that heaven will be even better! And one of the best things about our earthly life is our family. It's the place that we love and laugh, and grow and know. So today let's think about heaven as a giant family hug! Everybody find your family and have a group hug.

Children and families: (*Hugs*)

L: That's great. Congregation, why don't you stand up and hug someone near you too; it doesn't even matter if they're not in your family, because in Jesus we're one big family, right?

That was great! Let's have a prayer and thank God for the little taste of heaven we can have on earth in our families . . . (*prayer*).

—*Brant D. Baker*

Meet John Clearview

Scripture: Hebrews 11:1; Matthew 28:20

Season/Sunday: Any

Focus: Faith is the assurance of things hoped for and the conviction of things not seen, including the hope and conviction that God is everywhere, and always with us.

Experience: To celebrate God's presence and remember the promise Jesus made to be with us always, even to the end of the age; and to experience an act of believing.

Arrangements: You will want to become very familiar with the John Clearview routine. Rehearse so that you can do it naturally, adding your own words and inflexions to the routine. For helpful hints, watch the old Jimmy Stewart movie *Harvey*. He makes you believe he is talking with a six-foot white invisible rabbit.

Also, arrange with a helper to open a nearby door on cue. This person needs to stay out of sight, so that the door appears to open by itself.

Leader:	Good morning, boys and girls. How are you this morning?
Children:	Fine. Good.
L:	I'm glad you are! Say, I want you to meet someone (*look around as if you are expecting someone, then spot him and smile and wave*). There he is! Hello! (*Wave and head towards the back of the sanctuary to greet your mysterious guest. As you reach the middle of the sanctuary, stop and shake hands and then escort your guest down the aisle toward the children.*) I'm so glad you made it. . . . Oh no, you're not late; you're just in time. . . . Yes, yes it is a lovely sanctuary, isn't it (*continue making small talk with your friend until you are back with the children*)?
C:	There's no one there!

L: What? Yes, there is. I'd like you to meet a very special friend of mine. His name is John Clearview (*make a grand gesture of introduction*). He lives at 0001 Transparent Boulevard, but he has made a special trip to see you today. (*Children are likely giggling.*) What's wrong?

C: There is nobody there!

L: Well, sure there is . . . (*looking at John*). No, John, I'll handle this. (*Addressing children*) What makes you think no one is there?

C: Because you can't see him. 'Cause there's nobody there.

L: Well, hmm, you have a point there. John is kind of hard to see. Do you know why he is so difficult to see?

C: He's invisible!

L: That's right, he is an invisible man. I wonder what it's like to be invisible. Let's ask John. (*Turning to John*) John, what's it like to be invisible? (*Showing a look of surprise, then turning toward the children*) Why, he said people act like he is not even there! (*Turning back to John*) What? . . . No way! . . . Really? (*Turning to children*) He said folks don't wave when they go by, and don't say "excuse me" when they bump into him, and sometimes even step on his feet and walk right on past. (*Turning to John*) Well, that's not going to happen here! (*To the children*) Right?

C: Right!

L: Well, thanks, John for helping us learn a lesson about faith. What's that? . . . Oh, you have to go now? . . . Well, we understand. Come back soon. (*Watch John walk off toward the door where your helper is waiting.*) Hey, everybody, let's all turn and say goodbye to John.

All: Goodbye John! (*This is the cue for the door to open "by itself" and then close.*)

L: You know, John can help teach us something about faith. The Bible says that faith is the assurance of things hoped for, the conviction of things not seen.

Those are big words that mean that even though sometimes it seems like God is invisible, God is always there. Faith means that even though sometimes it's hard to see Jesus working in our lives, he is with us always. Faith means that sometimes we have to believe before we can see. Let's have a prayer and ask Jesus to help us have faith and remember that he is always with us . . . *(prayer)*.

—*Jeff Hutcheson*

Stand Firm

Scripture: 1 Corinthians 16:13; Ephesians 6:12-13;
2 Thessalonians 2:15; and Philippians 4:1

Season/Sunday: July 4

Focus: There may be no advice more often repeated from the apostle Paul than to "stand firm." He used the admonition in almost every letter he wrote, and in a variety of contexts. Using our national Independence Day celebration as a backdrop, this sermon focuses on how we can best "stand firm" when we stand together.

Experience: The children will watch others trying to stand firm, and then stand firm themselves as a group.

Arrangements: You will need two helpers. Since no rehearsal is required, you might be able to pick these from the congregation on the spot; but be sure they are fairly able-bodied so as not to lose their balance too easily. Also, have the scriptures used in the sermon readily marked in a Bible or printed on a sheet of paper. If time is a consideration, the leader can move directly from one person to the group (*leaving out the 2 Thessalonians reading*).

Leader: Good morning, and great to see you. I want to read a Bible verse to you, "Keep alert, <u>stand firm</u> in your faith, be courageous, be strong" (1 Corinthians 16:13). Who knows what it means to "stand firm"?

Children: To stand up? To be strong?

L: Yes, I think that's right, and I'm going to call on John Hee to come up here and help me demonstrate this. (*As volunteer arrives*) John, can you stand as firm and strong as you can, and be ready and brave?

John: I'll try, but I may only be able to do one thing at a time!

L: Let me know when you're ready.

64

John: I'm ready, I think.

L: (*Assess which way the volunteer is the strongest—probably front to back—and then push in that direction. Then go to the weak side and gently push the volunteer off balance.*) Whoops, looks like you're strong front to back, but not so strong side to side!

John: Yes, but I'm brave that way.

L: Okay, good. Well, let's read another Bible verse, "So then, brothers and sisters, <u>stand firm</u> and hold fast to the traditions that you were taught" (2 Thessalonians 2:15). What does it mean to hold fast to traditions?

C: To remember. To do things the old-fashioned way.

L: Right, to hold fast means to hold onto. I'm thinking that traditions, things we learned to do and keep on doing, that these involve other people, maybe people from long ago or someone from our time. Let's see, we need another person, a traditional person, to help John. Okay, let's ask Mr. Verch to help us. Todd, would you come up here, and perhaps you and John could stand firm together (*the two men arrange themselves in some way*). Okay, are you ready? Are you holding fast to your traditions?

Men: We think so!

L: (*Again assess their strength and test that, and then their vulnerability, which will probably still be from the side, and gently knock them off balance.*) Okay, still not as firm as it needs to be. Let's see what else the Bible says. Here's an interesting one from Ephesians, "For our struggle is not against enemies of blood and flesh, but against the rulers, against the authorities, against the cosmic powers of this present darkness, against the spiritual forces of evil in the heavenly places. Therefore take up the whole armor of God, so that you may be able to withstand on that evil day, and having done everything, to <u>stand firm</u>" (Ephesians 6:12-13). Wow. Paul makes it sound like we're in a pretty serious battle, and we need to be equipped. You guys start putting on your armor, and I wonder if we need to be thinking about an army here? What do you all think?

C: Yeah! Pick me.

L: How about you, and would you help too (*pick two children*)? Let's have the four of you get into some arrangement where you think you're armored and standing firm (*probably will resemble a huddle*). Ready?

Group: Yes!

L: (*At this point you shouldn't be able to topple them, nor do you want to push so hard that you do!*) Wow, that is firm! But how will you see your enemy, or even a friend, if you're all looking inward at one another? Why don't we all get into the group, but instead of facing inward, let's all face to the side so that we can look both inward at one another and outward, and as a group be standing firm. While you do that I'll read one more Bible verse, "Therefore, my brothers and sisters, whom I love and long for, my joy and crown, stand firm in the Lord in this way" (Philippians 4:1).

That looks like a good strong group, a group that is standing firm! Good job, and while you're all there let's have a prayer that as a church, and as a nation, we can only stand firm when we stand together . . . (*prayer*).

—*Brant D. Baker*

Cooking with Jesus (One)

Scripture: Matthew 28:16-20

Season/Sunday: Any

Focus: The Great Commission tells us to go and make disciples. It takes the right ingredients in the right mixture. This sermon looks at those various "ingredients" it takes to make a disciple.

Experience: The children will work on a "recipe" that includes Bible study, prayer, and Christians who love us to make disciples.

Arrangements: Mixing bowls, spoons, whisks, and other kitchen utensils used for mixing cakes or batters. A table for all these mixing items might help. You'll also need a "cook book" . . . a Bible!

Leader: Good morning. How is everyone today?

Children: Great!

L: That's good! Today we are going to make disciples. What is a disciple?

C: (*May or may not know.*)

L: A disciple is a follower of Jesus Christ, someone who wants to know his forgiveness and live a life of thankful response doing what Jesus wants us to do. So, does anyone know how to make a disciple?

C: No!

L: Well, I thought not, so I brought some bowls and spoons and whisks (*distribute items to children*). OK, so let's get started making our disciples. You mix up some disciple powder in that bowl there; and you can whisk whatever it is you have in that bowl; and I'll just keep stirring away right here. . . . (*Looking into the bowl*) Wait, I don't see any disciples. Hmmm, do you think we can make disciples like this?

C: No!

L: You can't? Oh no! How could we find out how to make them?

C: Ask somebody.

L: We could ask somebody, or, I know! We could find a recipe. Do you think there might a recipe in a cookbook somewhere?

C: No! Yes.

L: The recipe is in a special cookbook called our Bible *(getting Bible)*. Let's see what my Bible says. After Jesus rose from the dead, when he left the tomb, he spent some time with his disciples. Then, before he went back to heaven, he gave them some instructions. Let's read Matthew 28:16-20 *(read text, emphasizing the word <u>make</u> as you are reading)*.
See? Jesus said to <u>make</u> disciples. So maybe you don't make disciples the way you make a cake, but it must be that you need to put in some ingredients. What ingredients do you think it takes to make a disciple?

C: Reading the Bible. Praying. Coming to church. Helping people.

L: Wow, those are really good answers! Let's stand up and do some motions to help us remember each one of those. Reading the Bible *(leader and children put hands together like a book and read)*; praying *(hands clasped in prayer)*; coming to church *(walk in place)*; and helping people *(reach out toward one another or other worshipers)*.
That was great! Let's have a prayer and ask God to put all these ingredients in us and help us mix them up just right . . . *(prayer)*.

—*Kathleen Harris*

68

Cooking with Jesus (Two)

Scripture: 1 Corinthians 12:12-20

Season/Sunday: Any

Focus: This sermon looks at the fact that we all have a special ingredient (a spiritual gift) to contribute, and that we need to use those gifts together in order to make something tasty (unity in the body of Christ).

Experience: The sermon will showcase the ingredients that go into making a basic brownie recipe, which are useful but not really all that tasty alone, but together combine to make a great-tasting brownie. (This also makes a good Sunday school lesson if you have the time and kitchen facilities to have the kids help you make and bake the brownies. To do this, pre-measure and divide up your raw ingredients so that each child can add his or her "special ingredient," then bake per directions.)

Arrangements: You will need to prep the following and put into a cardboard box:

1. Pan of pre-cut brownies. It is best if they are in individual serving bags and enough for each child—for your convenience a recipe is included. If your church discourages eating in the sanctuary, be sure to mention to the children to wait until after worship to enjoy their treat.
2. A trash bag and some paper towels
3. The following raw ingredients each in its own sealed clear bag:
   - A raw egg broken in bag
   - Some oil and flour
   - Some salt, sugar, a touch of vanilla, & butter (mashed together)
   - Unsweetened chocolate chips or a bar coarsely chopped (unsweetened is important! Ideally enough so each child can have a small taste).

Leader: How many of you want to eat some brownies (*holding up your cardboard box*)?

Children: I do! Me!

L: OK . . .(*reaching into box, pulling out the bag with the raw egg and holding it up like it's a dirty sock*). Who wants to eat these raw eggs?

C: Not me!

L: But I thought you wanted some brownies. Don't eggs go into brownies? OK . . . (*reaching into box and pulling out bag with oil and flour*), who wants some vegetable oil and some flour to wash down those eggs?

C: Not me!

L: Oh, but oil and flour are important parts of brownies too. OK . . . (*reaching into box and pulling out bag with salt, sugar, and butter*), this doesn't look brownies either, does it? Who would want to eat this strange combination of salt, sugar, and butter? I think I'd rather have the brownies, wouldn't you?

C: Yes!

L: Well those are almost all of the ingredients for the brownies, but these brownies still seem to be missing something; what else do you think our brownies might need?

C: Chocolate?

L: That's right, brownies need chocolate; . . . let's see if I have some. (*Bring out bag with unsweetened chocolate chips.*) I do! Would anyone like some chocolate?

C: Me! Me too!

L: (*Distribute chocolate. Since it's unsweetened, it'll taste pretty bad.*) How does that taste?

C: Yucky!

L: I thought so (*this might be the time for the trash bag and paper towels*). We still seem to be missing something, don't we? We've got all the ingredients for brownies, but they don't taste very good by themselves, do they? What do you think we can do to turn these ingredients into brownies?

C: Mix them together!

L: That's right. . . . All alone these ingredients don't always taste very good, but together they make yummy brownies. You know, we are the same way. The Bible tells us that we each have a special ingredient that God has given to us . . . like this butter and sugar (*hold up bag and then drop back into box, repeat with each of the following*) . . . this chocolate . . . this egg . . . and the oil and flour. When we each give God our special ingredient . . . (*pretend to mix the contents of the box*) and let God bake them together in the heat of the Holy Spirit, we can work together to make good things for God, like our brownies here . . . (*pull out a brownie*).

C: Wow! Yummy!

L: Before we eat these, let's have a prayer and give thanks that God gives us each a special gift, a special ingredient, to mix together to make something good . . . (*prayer*). Now who would like a brownie?

C: Me!

Ben's Basic Brownie:
¼ cup butter
¼ cup vegetable oil
2 eggs
2 ounces unsweetened chocolate
1 cup sugar
2 teaspoons vanilla
¾ cup flour
¼ teaspoon salt

In saucepan over low heat, combine butter, oil, sugar, salt, and chocolate, and stir until melted and smooth. Remove pan from heat and mix in eggs and vanilla, then mix in the flour. Pour mixture in a greased 8x8x2-inch pan. Bake at 325° F for about 30 minutes or until done. Cool and cut. Makes about 24 brownies.

—*Benjamin Keller*

The Conversion of Saul

Scripture: Acts 9

Season/Sunday: Any

Focus: This sermon looks at the power of God to change lives—even lives that are already committed to God!

Experience: The children will all become the person of "Saul" in this reading and will enact Saul's responses as the story is read.

Arrangements: This children's sermon is a little more involved then some, and should perhaps be used on a Sunday when (1) the leader has time to pull it together and (2) time isn't too crucial an issue. You will need three adult helpers: a narrator, a "voice of Jesus," and someone to be Ananias. Of these, only Ananias needs to have generally memorized the few lines below; the others can use the script. Be sure to attend to microphone issues for all three of these people—a hands-free microphone for Ananias would be preferable. The children's sermon leader should help children make appropriate responses as suggested in the script.

> **Leader:** Good morning! Today we're going to hear a story about a man named Saul, but not only are we going to hear the story, we're going to pretend we're Saul. You may know Saul by a different name—he would become the apostle Paul. But let's listen to his story before he received his new name.
>
> **Narrator:** Saul was a man who lived a long time ago and loved God very much.
>
> **Children/Leader:** (*Raise hands to the heavens or bow in prayer to show love toward God.*)
>
> **Narrator:** But Saul had missed what God was doing and believed that the Christians were disobeying God's commands. He was so angry about it he decided to

get them arrested, and went on a trip to a city called Damascus to find any Christians living there.

Children/Leader: (*Show angry faces, and begin moving down an aisle toward "Damascus"—probably the narthex or area at the far end of the aisle.*)

Narrator: While Saul was on the way to Damascus, suddenly a bright light from heaven flashed around him. Saul fell to the ground (*children should all fall down*) and then heard a voice saying to him,

Voice of Jesus: Saul, why are you persecuting me?

Narrator: Saul didn't know. He asked, "Who are you, Lord?"

Children/Leader: (*Together say*) "Who are you, Lord?"

Voice of Jesus: I am Jesus, the one you are trying to hurt. Now here's what you are to do: get up and go to Damascus, and there someone will come and tell you what to do.

Narrator: The people who were traveling with Saul stood there speechless because they also heard the voice from heaven but saw no one.

Leader: (*Encourage nearby worshipers to react by putting hands over mouths and showing astonishment.*)

Narrator: Saul got up from the ground (*children get up*) and realized he couldn't see anything (*children should be encouraged to grope around*). That meant that the ones traveling with him had to lead him by the hand and take him into Damascus.

Leader: (*Engage nearby worshipers to get up and lead children to "Damascus." Once they all arrive, children should sit down and worshipers can be motioned to return to their seats.*)

Narrator: Saul was there for three days, unable to see, and during that same time he chose not to eat or drink anything either. Now there was a Christian disciple in Damascus named Ananias. And Jesus came to Ananias in a vision and called to him. . . .

Voice of Jesus: Ananias!

Ananias: (*Appearing "from nowhere"—perhaps from narthex or sitting in a pew near "Damascus"*) Here I am, Lord.

Voice of Jesus: Get up and go to Straight Street, and at the house of Judas ask for a man named Saul. He is praying right now, and I have given him a vision that you will come and lay hands on him so that he can see again.

Ananias: Lord, I've heard about this man, and I know he's here to arrest any of us who believe in you.

Voice of Jesus: It's okay, Ananias. Saul is the man I have chosen to take my name to many, many people. Go.

Narrator: So Ananias went and found the house and laid his hands on Saul (*Ananias should move near children and stretch out hands over all of them*).

Ananias: Brother Saul, the Lord Jesus who appeared to you on your way here has sent me so that you may regain your sight and be filled with the Holy Spirit.

Narrator: And right away it was as though scales fell from his eyes, and Saul was able to see again (*children react to being able to see*). And Saul got up and was baptized.

Leader: Wow! What a great story about how God works in people's lives! Let's have a prayer and give thanks for that, and for the work of Saul, who became Paul . . . (*prayer*).

—*Brant D. Baker*

Come (and Go!)

Scripture: Matthew 4:18-22 (NLT)

Season/Sunday: Any

Focus: Jesus' invitation to his disciples is an invitation into a relationship. Just as he invited those first disciples to come into a partnership, so he still calls and invites us to come to him today. Of course, eventually in the Gospel narrative Jesus also tells the disciples to go. That might not feel like a relational gesture, but even as he tells them to go he promises to be with them.

Experience: The children and the leader will move around the sanctuary to experience "coming" and "going."

Arrangements: None are needed, but be sure you use the words "come" and "go" often and with lots of emphasis!

Leader: I would like to invite the children to <u>come</u> and join me in the front of the sanctuary. I am so glad you could <u>come</u> and join me. Now that we are all settled in, I would like you all to get up and <u>go</u> to the back of the sanctuary (*direct them to a specific spot, for example, the back doors, the center aisle, or near the last pew*).

Children: (*Move to spot indicated.*)

L: You did a great job following instructions, but now you are so far away from me. Maybe I just need to <u>come</u> to where you are so we will be together (*move to join children*). Now that we are all together, <u>come</u> with me to the front of the sanctuary, and let's sit down there.

C: This is a lot of exercise!

L: (*As you reassemble*) Today our Bible story tells about a time when Jesus invited some people to <u>come</u> and follow him. The men were busy doing their work as fishermen, catching fish to sell in the markets. Jesus

said to them, " 'Come, be my disciples, and I will show you how to fish for people!' And they left their nets at once and went with him. A little farther up the shore he saw two other brothers, James and John, sitting in a boat with their father, Zebedee, mending their nets. And he called them to come, too. They immediately followed him, leaving the boat and their father behind" (Matthew 4:19-22).
When I told you to come to the front of the church, we were very close. When I told you to go, did it seem as if we were close?

C: No!

L: When I came to join you in the back of the church, were we closer?

C: Yes!

L: So we might say that when we are invited to come, it is a time to be close, like what Jesus did with Simon, Andrew, James, and John in our story today. Jesus invites them to come, and they get to be close with Jesus. When you invite friends to come to your house to play, you get to be close to them. When people invite you to come to eat, you get to be close to them. Jesus invited the fishermen to come be with him, and they learned some wonderful things and got to know Jesus as the Son of God. That happened because they came when he invited them to come. Did you know that Jesus still calls us to come? What happens when we come to Jesus?

C: We get close to him!

L: That's right! When we come to Jesus, we get to be a little closer to God. And then, Jesus also asks us to go, to go out into the world, to go to people who need our help, to go and share the good news of how God wants people to come. And, it's also good news that no matter if we are coming or going, our Lord is with us! Let's have a prayer and ask Jesus to help us come to him every day . . . *(prayer)*.

—*Paula Hoffman*

God Is Real

Scripture: Psalm 115:3-7

Season/Sunday: Any

Focus: God is real and alive, and working in our lives.

Experience: To celebrate and give praise for God's realness. To experience the difference between something manufactured and "the real thing."

Arrangements: You will need a toy dog (or some other pet of your choice). A helper to assist in reading the verses from Psalm 115 will help free you to concentrate on the hand motions.

> **Leader:** (*Carrying the toy pet with you as you greet the children.*) Good morning! I'd like you to meet my pet doggie, Chewy (*gently petting the dog as if it were real*). I love my little Choo-choo. She's so sweet.
>
> **Children:** (*Giggles.*)
>
> **L:** She doesn't eat too much, and hardly ever barks. I love my dog.
>
> **C:** That's not a real dog.
>
> **L:** It's not?!
>
> **C:** No.
>
> **L:** Why not?
>
> **C:** 'Cause it can't bark. It can't run.
>
> **L:** Well, you have a good point there, and you're right: this isn't a real dog. I was showing you this because sometimes people make a statue or some kind of carving and worship it as though it were a real god and had real powers. But the God we worship is a real God. The Bible teaches us that God is real and loves us and can really do things on our behalf. In the Bible there is a description of our real living God, and our helper Kellen is going to read from Psalm 115 (*author paraphrase*) while we do some hand

motions together. Let's stand up; in fact, let's have the whole congregation stand up, and then you do what I do!

Helper: "Our God is in the heavens, and does whatever he pleases. But the people of the world have idols; idols made of things people think have value. These idols have mouths, but they can't speak."

Leader and All: (*Open and close mouths as if trying to say something.*)

    H: "They have eyes, but they can't see."

Leader and All: (*Put hands out in front as if groping in the dark.*)

    H: "They have ears, but they do not hear."

Leader and All: (*Cup hand behind ear as if trying to hear.*)

    H: "They have noses, but they can't smell."

Leader and All: (*Sniff the air, and then shrug shoulders in defeat.*)

    H: "They have hands, but they can't clap."

Leader and All: (*Try to clap but miss.*)

    H: "They have feet, but they don't walk."

Leader and All: (*Pulling up on legs as if trying to make them move.*)

    H: "They can't even make a noise in their throat."

Leader and All: (*Put hand to throat and open mouth but with no sound.*)

    L: Wow! Would you want to worship a god like that?

    C: No!

    L: Me neither! Let's pray to our God who is real, and who really hears us and speaks to us and loves us . . . (*prayer*).

—Jeff Hutcheson

Friends of Jesus

Scripture: John 15:15

Season/Sunday: Any

Focus: To discover ways to deepen our friendship with Jesus.

Experience: The children will be encouraged to think about activities that deepen their earthly friendships and then about how those apply to their friendship with Jesus.

Arrangements: The main answer that the children are likely to give to the question "How do we become friends?" is "Play." As mentioned in the introduction, if the children don't supply the needed answer, feel free to supply it yourself. The sermon below uses the game of "patty cake" as a "hand-clap and sing" type of game. After giving the children this experience, you then need to lead them in singing "This Is the Day" or some similar simple song they and you might know, accompanied by hand clapping. If you are not comfortable leading this, you might invite someone to help you. You might also want to prompt the choir to help lead the echo if you use the suggested song. If time is a concern, the leader may want to skip the back-scratching step suggested below.

Leader: Good morning! Great to see everyone today, and I have a question for you. What are the names of some of your friends?

Children: Sam, Julie, Tamara, Justin. . .

L: Wow! You all have a lot of friends! And what are some of the ways that you get to be better friends? What are some of the things you do together?

C: Play!

L: That's right, we play together. So let's stand up, and let's play a game of patty cake. Everyone find a partner, and let's clap our hands together like this (*demonstrate*) and say, "Patty cake, patty cake, baker's man. Bake me a cake as fast as you can. Roll

79

it (*pretend rolling*) and pat it (*make patting motion*) and mark it with B (*make a B in the air or on the back of your hand*), and put it in the oven for baby and me (*clapping*).

That was great! Well, let me ask you another question. You named some of your friends, but is Jesus our friend too?

C: Yes!

L: That's right, and how do you suppose we might become better friends with him? Could we find a way to play with him too?

C: (*Uncertain.*)

L: (*Start clapping to set rhythm and begin singing*) "This is the day (*children and congregation echo*), This is the day (*echo*), that the Lord has made (*echo*), that the Lord has made (*echo*), Let us rejoice (*echo*), let us rejoice (*echo*), and be glad in it (*echo*), and be glad in it (*echo*). (*Together*) This is the day that the Lord has made; let us rejoice and be glad in it. This is the day (*echo*), this is the day (*echo*), that the Lord has made" [from *Scripture in Song* by Les Garrett]. That was great! So playing with Jesus by singing and clapping, just as with our other friends, is a way for us to become better friends with him. How else do you become better friends with someone?

C: (*Depending on ages may get stuck on other games they play; if so prompt as follows.*)

L: Do you ever do something nice for them, like maybe scratch their backs (*scratch someone's back nearby*), and then ask them to scratch your back (*encourage children to play along scratching each other's backs*)? We help each other, right? How could we help Jesus? What do Jesus' arms look like?

C: Like this (*showing arms*)!

L: Well, that's exactly right; Jesus' arms look like our arms because they are our arms! So sometimes we can help Jesus by doing something he would want done, like . . . giving some of these people a hug! Look at these people (*leading children to congregation*), they really look like they need a hug from

Jesus; can you give them a hug? *(Get everyone hugging, including yourself!)*
Okay, last question, do you ever become better friends with someone by talking with them?

C: Yes!

L: Of course! And what do we call it when we talk with Jesus? *(Bring hands together in posture of prayer if no one calls out the answer right away.)*

C: Prayer!

L: So let's all join hands now and talk with our friend Jesus . . . *(prayer).*

—*Brant D. Baker*

Under Construction

Scripture: Hebrews 12:1

Season/Sunday: Any, although this sermon would work well with a baptism.

Focus: We are all indebted to those who have gone before, to the men and women who have given of themselves, often in ways we never know about.

Experience: The children will be introduced to men and women of faith, all of whom surround the children in such a way as to help them as they are "under construction."

Arrangements: Procure the yellow tape used at construction sites with the words "Under Construction" on it and cut lengths that include those words, or make your own small yellow signs with the same words. You will need enough to give one to every child. A helper with some tape might speed up the process (although another option is to generate these on a computer and print to a nametag). You will also need to think through a list of three or four people who volunteer for various jobs around the church. Look for the people who serve quietly, whom others might really not know about: the gardeners, the money counters, administrators, and so forth. Every church has members who have been quietly doing jobs around the church for years. It is fun to surprise them, but you will need to make sure they are in attendance that Sunday.

Leader: Good morning. How is everyone today?
Children: Good!
L: I'm so glad. Today I am going to introduce you to some good people in our church. Some of them you might know, but others you might not. Meet Howard. Did you know that he has counted money from the offering for twenty-five years? Every Monday morning, he counts the nickels and pennies

82

and dollars that are given to the church. Let's say "thank you" to Mr. Frey.

C: Thank you, Mr. Frey!

L: Next meet Isabel. Did you know that she is the lady who plants and takes care of the flowers in the flowerbeds in the front of the church? Don't they look pretty? Let's say "thank you" to Mrs. Santos.

C: Thank you, Mrs. Santos!

L: Next I want you to meet Clyde. Did you know that he has stood at the door for twenty years and greeted people as they come to church? That's a lot of greeting! Let's say "thanks" to Clyde.

C: Thanks, Clyde!

L: It takes all of these people and more to make everything happen around the church that needs to happen. But what about us? We're just kids, can we do those jobs?

C: No.

L: No, but that's okay (*begin distributing "Under Construction" signs*). Maybe we can do a few things, but mostly right now we are "Under Construction!" Not only that, but all of these people in the congregation are the ones who help us and fit us and form us. They are what the Bible calls "a great cloud of witnesses," who will help you all grow up to be the future planters and counters and greeters. As far as that goes, I'm not so sure I'm not "under construction" too—give me one of those . . . ! (*Be sure every child has a sign and then close with prayer.*)

—Kathleen Harris

A Letter from Paul

Scripture: 1 Timothy 1:1-3 (and the first lines of virtually any of Paul's letters)

Season/Sunday: Any

Focus: Most of the New Testament, as we have it, is in the form of letters.

Experience: The children will experience what it could be like to receive a letter from Paul.

Arrangements: You will need to prepare a letter ahead of time. It can be short and should be handwritten. Make sure it is signed "Paul" in big letters at the bottom. You will also need a helper to deliver the letter as you begin, as though it just arrived.

Leader: Good morning, boys and girls!
Children: Good morning!
L: I wonder how many of you have ever gotten a letter in the mail? Anybody?
C: Me. Me too. I got one from my aunt for my birthday; she sent money.
L: Ooh. Money letters are always nice. Well, today we're going to talk about what is in the Bible . . . (*cue for mail person to come down the aisle waving the letter*).
Helper: Excuse me! Pardon me!
L: What is this?
H: (*Out of breath . . .*) This just arrived for the children.
L: (*Looking surprised*) For the children! Well, thank you (*helper hurries off*). Should we open it?
C: Yea!
L: (*Opening letter*) "Dear Children of _____ (*your church name*), Grace and peace to you. I hope

this letter finds you well. I am writing to tell you how special and wonderful you are. You are God's precious children. Don't ever forget that. Jesus loves you so much, and so do I! Keep the faith! Signed . . ." Whose name is that?

C: The apostle Paul.

L: Wow! You got a letter from Paul. It must have been lost in the mail for quite some time! Well, that's exactly what I wanted to talk about today. Did you know that most of the New Testament is letters? That's right, letters, similar to this one. And do you know who wrote most of them?

C: Jesus? God? Paul?

L: Those are all good answers! Paul wrote many of the letters, but he was writing to encourage other people, to help them keep the faith, and most of all, to let them know how much Jesus loved them. Say, I have an idea! Do you see many mailboxes when you're out driving around with your mom and dad, or out playing?

C: Yes! We have a mailbox.

L: Since you may not get many more letters from Paul, what if you decided to think about how much Jesus loves you every time you see a mailbox? That would be a lot of love! Will you try it this week?

C: Yes!

L: Okay! Well, let's have a prayer and thank God that Jesus loves us so much . . . *(prayer)*. (*You might want to display the letter from Paul for a week or so on a bulletin board somewhere around the church where the children will see it.*)

—*Jeff Hutcheson*

How Old Are You?

Scripture: Proverbs 20:29

Season/Sunday: Any will work, but Grandparents' Day would be ideal (the first Sunday after Labor Day).

Focus: This sermon strives to show how we can gain wisdom as we age, and that our image of God can grow and mature.

Experience: The children will meet and hear from a variety of successfully older members of the church, who will share their wisdom on the nature of God.

Arrangements: No special arrangements are necessary, although you may want to think through the age groupings likely to be present in worship. Beyond that the leader simply needs to know two questions to ask each person: (1) "What is the best part of being your present age?" and (2) "What is your current image of God?" The leader will need to rephrase the answer to the second question into an easily repeated affirmation of faith. The leader should use some judgment in who is interviewed from each age group, choosing someone who will be able to give a coherent response. If the leader doesn't know the people that well, or if the congregation is not comfortable with providing answers on-the-spot, the leader may want to contact people the week ahead so they can be thinking about their answers.

Leader:	Will the children please come forward? Come on. Good to see everybody today. Got to stand up. We have places to go, people to see, things to do. Yep. Yep. Yep. Good to see everybody. All right. I have a question before we go on a little trip here. How old is old? When you think of somebody that's old, what do you think of?
Child:	Like 100.
Leader:	Like 100? Okay. What do you think of?
Child:	92.

Leader: 92? Okay, and what about you?

Child: A thousand.

Leader: A thousand? Well, I don't know of anybody that's a thousand, but if you're a teenager or in your twenties, would you raise your hand? And we're just going to interview some people. You want to just mosey over here with me, and we'll talk to Kevin. So, Kevin . . .

Kevin: Yeah.

Leader: What's the best thing about being how old you are?

Kevin: I'm old enough to drive.

Leader: That's good! And what is your image of God? What's your image of God in about five to ten words?

Kevin: I dunno. The God on "The Simpsons" . . . big legs.

Leader: Big legs . . . big God.

Kevin: Yeah.

Leader: Okay, let's all say together "God is big."

Children (and congregation): God is big.

Leader: Good, thanks, Kevin. Okay, if you're in your thirties or forties, would you please raise your hand? Hmmm . . . some of you are stretching this a little bit, I think; but we're not going to do an ID check. Let's go over here and talk to Pam (*moving*). Pam?

Pam: Yes.

Leader: We won't ask how old you are, but these children want to know what's the best thing about being how old you are.

Pam: No, you can ask; I'm 46. And the best thing about being 46 is that I don't have to ask anybody's permission.

Leader: Could be some advantages there! And what's your image or concept of God?

Pam: My concept of God is something that's all around me and inside me.

Leader: Okay, let's all say together "God is all around."

Children (and congregation): God is all around.

Leader: Great, thank you. Now, if you're in your fifties or sixties, would you please raise your hand? Now these are the people that are really honest, and we appreciate

your honesty. Let's go over here and talk to my friend
Kim. What's the best part of being your age, Kim?

Kim: It's a great time of life. Maturity is good.

Leader: Good answer—and your image of God at this time in
your life?

Kim: God is the true father.

Leader: So let's all say together, "God is the true father."

Children (and congregation): God is the true father.

Leader: Nice, thank you. And now let's ask people in their
seventies or eighties to raise their hand. (*Moving*)
Let's go back up here in the middle because I've
determined that the older you are in this church, the
closer you sit to the center. Let's go talk to my friend
Mary. Mary, what's the best part about being the age
that you are right now?

Mary: Probably having a little more wisdom and a little
more understanding.

Leader: More wisdom and more understanding—good. And
what is your image of God?

Mary: Love, compassion, and strength.

Leader: Let's all say it together, "God is love, compassion,
and strength."

Children (and congregation): God is love, compassion, and
strength.

Leader: Beautiful. Let's go to the top, anyone who is ninety
or beyond (*moving*). Hi, Margaret. How are you?

Margaret: I'm fine.

Leader: I wouldn't think you a day over 79.

Margaret: Thank you. That's a compliment.

Leader: What's the best part of being in your nineties?

Margaret: That I've been able to do all the things I have.

Leader: And what's your image or concept of God at this
time of your life?

Margaret: I think God is somebody who is very loving, who
accepts all the crazy things I do and still loves me.

Leader: You still do crazy things? We'll talk later. For now,
let's all say together, "God always loves us."

Children (and congregation): God always loves us.

Leader: Well, now that you've heard from all these different
ages, what age would you rather be?

Children: *(Offer various ages, one says his own age, three.)*
Leader: Three? That's how old you are. Perfect! Let's hold
hands and have a prayer and thank God that we can
gain wisdom as we get older, and that no matter
what age we are, God loves us . . . *(prayer).*

—*Brant D. Baker*

Growing Up and Increasing

Scripture: Mark 4:1-9

Season/Sunday: Back to School

Focus: At the start of another school year, this sermon will lead the children to think about the things that will help them grow fruitfully.

Experience: The children will talk about what a plant needs in order to grow, and will then act out the parable of the sower. Finally, they will discuss what they need to grow this school year.

Arrangements: You will need a Bible, a healthy-looking plant, and an unhealthy-looking plant. An adult helper is needed to narrate the parable while the leader guides the acting.

Leader: Good morning! (*Bring out the unhealthy-looking plant.*) Oh no. This plant doesn't look so good. It looks a little sick. What do you think happened?

Children: You didn't water it enough. It needs sun. It's dying.

L: You're probably right. So, you're saying that a plant needs water and sunshine. Anything else? What else does a plant need in order to grow tall and strong?

C: Love. Food. My mommy kills her plants too. Good dirt.

L: All those are good answers. It's so sad that this plant did not get all the things you just said. I will have to take it home and take better care of it! (*Put away the unhealthy plant.*)
This morning, I want to share a parable with you. Parables are special stories that Jesus told to teach people special lessons. Will you help me tell the story?

C: Yes!

L: Super! Let's start by standing up. This parable is from the Gospel of Mark in the New Testament, chapter 4 verses 1-9. (*Open Bible to Mark 4.*) Jesus began to teach beside the lake. The crowd got so big that Jesus had to get into a boat on the lake. So Jesus taught from the lake, while all the people sat on the land. This is what Jesus said:

Narrator: "Listen! A sower went out to sow. And as he sowed, some seed fell on the path."

L and C: Children, let's pretend we are some of the seeds the sower just planted (*fall down to the ground and sit in a ball.*)

N: Then "the birds came and ate it up."

L and C: Oh no, don't eat us! (*Have the children follow your hand gestures: cover your face as if you're protecting yourself from the birds.*)

N: "Other seed fell on rocky ground, where it did not have much soil, and it sprang up quickly, since it had no depth of soil."

L and C: Oh, the soil is too rocky here, and it's not deep enough. (Spring up quickly and stand up straight.)

N: "And when the sun rose, it was scorched; and since it had no root, it withered away."

L and C: (*While narrator is reading the previous line, block your eyes from the sun and fan yourself.*) Oh, the sun is bright and it is so hot. Oh, I'm so thirsty and weak. I'm dying. (*Wither away by "melting" your body and sitting back down.*)

N: "Other seed fell among thorns, and the thorns grew up and choked it, and it yielded no grain."

L and C: Ouch! These thorns are sharp (*pretend you are being pricked by thorns*). Ouch, oh, they're choking me! (*Bring your hands around your throat like you're choking.*)

N: "Other seed fell into good soil and brought forth grain, growing up and increasing and yielding thirty and sixty and a hundredfold."

L and C: Oh, this is nice dirt. Don't you like this dirt? It feels nice and rich (*feeling around you*). Oh, and look, we're growing (*stand up slowly*), and increasing (*continue to stand up until you are standing up straight*), and look at the thirty, sixty, and hundredfold of flowers that are growing off our branches (*bring out your arms and open your hands*).

N: And Jesus said, "Let anyone with ears to hear listen!"

L: That was a really fun parable. Would you want to be the seed on the path, on the rocky ground, among thorns, or on good soil?

C: The seed in good soil!

L: Why?

C: Because they grew. Because the other ones died. Because it was good dirt.

L: (*Bringing out healthy plant.*) Look at this healthy plant. I bet this plant has good soil, good sunlight, and just the right amount of water. I wonder what you think you need in order to grow strong and tall like this healthy plant as you start this new school year.

C: Food. Books.

L: Good answers. Anything else? Does anyone need love? What about plenty of rest? How about some dirt?!

C: Yes!

L: Well, this whole church is praying that all of you will grow and be fruitful this year. Let's pray right now . . . (*prayer*).

—*Joyce S. Fong*

Why We Read the Bible

Scripture: Romans 12:2

Season/Sunday: Any or Christian Education Sunday

Focus: The Bible changes our view of things; it stretches our imaginations, and helps us see the world more as God sees it. The Bible is a gift that helps us fulfill the call to be transformed by the renewing of our minds. It helps us to discern "what is the will of God—what is good and acceptable and perfect."

Experience: To experience a different view of the sanctuary and relate that to why we read the Bible. The Bible gives us a different view of our lives.

Arrangements: You will need a sturdy chair that you can stand on, a helper to help you and the children stand safely on the chair, and a Bible.

Leader: (*Standing on the chair*) Good morning! Do you know what I'm doing?

Children: Standing on a chair!

L: That's right. Can you guess why I am standing on this chair?

C: So you'll be taller? Because you're silly?

L: Nope. I'm standing up here because I want to get a different view of the sanctuary this morning. I want to get a different way of looking at our congregation. (*Looking around*) It sure does look different from up here. You want to take a look?

C: I do! (*With your helper assist as many children as are interested or as time allows, to stand on the chair and take a look around.*)

L: Do things look different from up there?

C: Yes! I can see everything.

L: It changes your whole point of view, doesn't it? Can you think of any other way to get a different way of looking at things (*holding up Bible to prompt answer*)?

C: Stand on the Bible?

L: Well, kind of. Not stand on it with our feet, but stand in it to know what it says and see things the way God sees things. That's another way of getting to see things differently. Reading the Bible is like standing on a chair or standing on your head. It gives us a different view of the world, and ourselves. It helps us see things more the way God might see them.

C: Can we stand on our heads?

L: Not right now. Let's pray and ask God to help us stand on the Bible to see things God's way . . . (*prayer*).

—*Jeff Hutcheson*

Witnesses

Scripture: Acts 1:8

Season/Sunday: Any, but this sermon would work well for an Evangelism Sunday.

Focus: This sermon will focus on the nature of the work of a witness: remembering, caring, and speaking.

Experience: To remember various events in the life and work of the church and to share them with the people closest to us, those a little more distant from us, and then to "all the world."

Arrangements: None are necessary, but you may want to think through what "good news" about your church you'd like to lead the children to proclaim, and what succinct phrase you might use to do so. For example, in the sermon below the proclamation is "free food" because the church has a food closet. Tailor the message to the mission available.

Leader: Good morning, and great to see you! Wow, so much is happening in our church that I have trouble remembering all the good things. Can you help me? What have you seen happen in our church that is really good?

Children: *(May or may not be able to respond without some prompting. Some possible ideas might include people worshiping, people praying, people caring—name specifics, people giving time and money to help others, and so forth.)*

L: Wow, those <u>are</u> some pretty wonderful things. Say, you know what, I think other people would want to know this. I mean, we all know it now, but don't you think we should tell someone else? Let's pick one of those things—let's pick the wonderful way that our deacons care for the people in our community by giving out food bags—and let's go tell those people there *(indicate a portion of the congregation)* and there *(indicate another portion)*. *(Help divide and distribute children, being sure they know the message.)*

C: Our deacons give away food.

L: *(Gathering children in center aisle)* Well okay, we told ourselves, we told some people close by. Hmmm, I think maybe we should tell <u>everybody</u>. What do you think *(making your way with children in tow toward the main sanctuary doors)*.

C: Yeah!

L: Yeah! We should tell everyone we can about this great way that we show people the love of Christ by giving away food. We could say, "Free food because we love Jesus!" *(Arriving at doors and taking children outside)* On the count of three let's yell that out as loud as we can, "Free food because we love Jesus." Are you ready? One, two, three . . .

C: Free food because we love Jesus!

L: That was a great proclamation, and a wonderful witness. And that's what God wants us to be all the time, witnesses who remember and care and tell others about the mighty acts of God. Let's have a prayer and ask God to help us do just that . . . *(prayer)*.

—*Brant D. Baker*

That They May All Be One

Scripture: John 17:20-26

Season/Sunday: World Communion Sunday (first Sunday in October)

Focus: Jesus' prayer is that all his followers be in unity, that they know "communion" not only with him but with one another as well.

Experience: To signify unity with one another, and with Christians around the world, by encircling the sanctuary, and joining hands in prayer. The leader can choose to pray extemporaneously or to use the great priestly prayer of Jesus from the upper room the night of the Last Supper (John 17:20-26).

Arrangements: Decide on the type of prayer to be offered. If you decide to use the scripture text, you'll need a Bible with you, or if you use the edited version below, a copy of that. Also, think through the anticipated logistics of encircling the worship space with worshipers joining hands. Do you need to use everyone? If not, consider making a comment on the ways in which God's people encircle all those around the world with their love and prayers. Or, do you anticipate having too few people to go around the entire perimeter? If so you may need to choose a smaller circumference (*one section of the worship space*).

> **Leader:** As the children come forward today, I'd like to invite everyone else to get up and move to the outside aisles. If you're in the back row there, or in the front row here, you can simply stand up—no need to move. Everyone else, up, up, up! (*Addressing the children*) Good morning! Do you know what special day it is?
>
> **Children:** Sunday? My auntie's birthday.
>
> **L:** Those are all good answers! But today is also a day called "World Communion Sunday." All around the

world today, Christians are making a special point to have communion. Why would they do that?

C: Because communion is special. Because Jesus said to.

L: Those are more good answers! And Jesus did say we should do this, not only to have a special union with him, a communion, but also to have a special union with one another. So, what we have here *(indicating all of the people standing around the sanctuary perimeter)* is the world. All of these people represent people all around the world. But I see some gaps, and that's where you come in. Each of you has been created by God to help fill in some special place in God's world. So, let's go out and fill in the gaps. . . . I see a big gap there between the choir and the people over there . . . *(and so on, directing children)*.

Now, you may notice that there are some people sitting inside our circle. What about them? If we all represent all the Christians around the world who are celebrating communion today, whom do the people sitting in the middle represent?

C: People who can't get to church? People who don't know Jesus?

L: Those are good answers! And we know that those people are certainly surrounded by the circle of God's love. Well, that's a beautiful circle. Let's join hands now, and I'll read a prayer based on the great priestly prayer that Jesus offered in the upper room the night of the Last Supper. Let us pray:

Gracious God, as our Lord Jesus prayed, so we pray, that we may all be one. As you, Lord God, are in Jesus and he in you, so may we also be in you, that the world may believe in your Son. Dear God, the glory that you have given your Son has also been given to us so that we may be unity with him and with one another. May this unity show all the world that you are perfect love, both in your triune self and in your love for all creation. May this love draw all people to you, Forgiving Lord, and may it strengthen us, as disciples of Jesus Christ, to go in his name to share the good news. Righteous Lord, we know the world does not know you, but because of your grace, we do. Make us bold in our proclamation of your great love, for we ask it in Jesus' name. Amen.

—*Brant D. Baker*

Let Everything That Breathes Praise the Lord! (Part One)

Scripture: Psalm 150

Season/Sunday: Any. Note that this is the first in a three-part series, but it is not necessary that the three parts be done on successive Sundays.

Focus: Anybody can praise God. We can praise God *anytime* we want. We can praise God with *anybody* we want. We can praise God *anywhere* we want. We can praise God in *any way* we want. Let everything that breathes praise the Lord.

Experience: The children will learn the different ways we can praise God. In this sermon they will use musical instruments.

Arrangements: You will need an assortment of musical instruments, such as tambourines, triangles, and drum sticks. Even whistles, pots and pans, and other types of noisemakers will do. Make sure you have enough for each child. A narrator or reader to say the verses from Psalm 150 will keep you free to direct the "orchestra."

Leader: Good morning! Wow, what a beautiful morning to praise the Lord! Let everything that breathes praise the Lord! Praise, praise, praise, I love praising the Lord. Children, what do you think it means to praise the Lord?

Children: Worship. Praise. Praying. Singing.

L: Those are all great answers! Praising God is how we thank God for all that God has done for us. It is a way for us to say something good about God like, "Wow, God. You are so good and powerful." But let me ask you a question: *when* is it okay to praise the Lord?

C: In the morning? Anytime?

L: Yes, we can praise God in the morning, at night, even in our dreams! And *who* can praise the Lord?

C: People. Kids. Parents.

L: Those are all great answers—and not only people, but the Bible says the animals, the plants, everything that has breath! Okay, *where* can we praise the Lord?

C: In church. At home.

L: That's right! We can praise God here in this sanctuary. We can praise the Lord in our homes. We can praise in the park or at the dinner table or even at school. God invites us to praise anywhere and everywhere! Okay, last question, *how* do we praise the Lord? What are some things we do here at church and at home to praise the Lord?

C: Sing. Pray. Preaching.

L: Yes! There are many ways we can praise the Lord! But there is one way you didn't mention—by playing instruments! (*Bring out your bag of instruments.*) I just happen to have a bag here that will help us praise God. Let's see what we have in here. (*Take out instruments and begin to distribute. It's probably not helpful to try and keep everyone quiet as they receive their instrument, and in fact not really necessary!*) Let's praise God with these. Does everyone have one? All right, let's have a concert of praising God. When I give you this signal, start playing (*show them the signal you will use*); and when I give you this signal (*show signal*), stop. Everyone ready? Let's practice (*do a few starts and stops*). Wow, you are fast learners! I bet God can't wait to hear us praise God with our music. Okay, here we go:

Narrator: Praise God "with trumpet sound;"

L: (*Signal children to play a few moments, then stop.*)

N: "Praise [God] with lute and harp!"

L: (*Signal start and stop.*)

N: "Praise [God] with tambourine and dance;"

L: (*Signal start and stop.*)

N: And "with strings and pipe!"

L: (*Signal start and stop.*)

N: Praise God "with clanging cymbals; . . . with loud clashing cymbals!"

L: (*Signal start and let the "music" continue for a bit*

longer this time, then signal to stop.) That was really great! Let's have a prayer and give thanks that God received all of that and all our praise, and that we can give praise in so many ways . . . *(prayer).*

—*Joyce S. Fong*

Let Everything That Breathes Praise the Lord! (Part Two)

Scripture: Psalm 150

Season/Sunday: Any. Note that this is the second in a three-part series, but it is not necessary that the three parts be done on successive Sundays.

Focus: Anybody can praise God. We can praise God *anytime* we want. We can praise God with *anybody* we want. We can praise God *anywhere* we want. We can praise God in *any way* we want. Let everything that breathes praise the Lord.

Experience: The children will learn the different ways we can praise God. In this sermon they will use their bodies.

Arrangements: None are needed, but be sure you are familiar with the hand motions you will use.

> **Leader:** Good morning! Today we're going to continue to look at the different ways we can praise God. Do you remember when we can praise God, who can praise God, and where we can praise God?
>
> **Children:** Anyone, everywhere, with noisy instruments!
>
> **L:** Those are all the right answers! The Bible tells us that everyone, everywhere, can praise God in just about every way! Today we're going to learn another way we can praise God, through the movements of our body. Psalm 150:4 says, "Praise [God] with . . . dance." Everybody stand up and let's start our dance by reaching for God *(start with your hands open and down beside your body, then raise your hands up high, like you're reaching for the sky).*
>
> **C:** *(Follow motion.)*
>
> **L:** Now let's open up our bodies to receive God's blessing. *(Bring your hands down to your shoulder level, stretched outward like a cross.)*
>
> **C:** *(Follow motion.)*

L: Now let's bring God's blessing into our hearts. (*Swoop hands together and clasp out in front of yourself, then bring the hands to the heart.*)

C: (*Follow motion.*)

L: Now let's thank God for God's blessing. (*Bring your hands away from your heart to a position of prayer. You may want to kneel down.*)

C: (*Follow motion.*)

L: Last, let's share this blessing with everyone. (*Swoop hands back out from the prayer position and spread outward from the body toward the congregation or one another.*)

C: (*Follow motion.*)

L: Wow, that was great! That was beautiful praising. Let's invite the congregation to be involved too. (*Invite congregation to stand, and together with children repeat motions. Since they won't be able to kneel, you might suggest that they sit instead.*)

Children and Congregation:

(*Follow motion with leader's verbal instruction.*)

L: That was wonderful! Let's do that one more time, this time in silence, and have that be our closing prayer . . . (*repeat sequence in silence*).

—Joyce S. Fong

Let Everything That Breathes Praise the Lord! (Part Three)

Scripture: Psalm 150

Season/Sunday: Any. Note that this is the third in a three-part series, but it is not necessary that the three parts be done on successive Sundays.

Focus: Anybody can praise God. We can praise God *anytime* we want. We can praise God with *anybody* we want. We can praise God *anywhere* we want. We can praise God in *any way* we want. Let everything that breathes praise the Lord.

Experience: The children will learn the different ways we can praise God. In this sermon they will use their voices. The sermon below also incorporates the use of instruments and bodies from the previous sermons of the series.

Arrangements: You will need to supply the instruments as you did in part 1, and it would again be helpful to have a narrator to do the reading.

Leader:	Good morning, and what a great day for everything that has breath to praise the Lord! We've been learning some of the ways to praise God—what have been your favorites so far?
Children:	Making noise!
L:	Well, I thought so! But did you know that even if you don't have anything to make noise with, and even if you can't use your body, there is something else you can use? Do you know what it is?
C:	Our hands? Our selves? Our voice?
L:	That's right, our voices are another way to praise God! Let's try that; everyone repeat after me, "Let everything that breathes . . ."
C:	"Let everything that breathes . . ."
L:	"praise the Lord."
C:	"praise the Lord!"

L: "Let everything that breathes praise the Lord!"

C: "Let everything that breathes praise the Lord!"

L: Awesome! Well, today we get to put together all of the ways we've learned to praise God. So first of all, here are the instruments again—everyone take one (*distribute*), and remember that this is the signal to start (*show signal from part 1*) and this is the signal to stop (*show signal*). Okay, to start this we don't need our instruments, so let's put those all down and be ready to use our bodies.

Narrator: "Praise the Lord!"

Leader and Children: (*Bring hands up to the sky.*)

N: "Praise God in [the] sanctuary;"

L and C: (*Bring hands to the side like a cross.*)

N: "Praise [the Lord] in [the] mighty firmament!"

L and C: (*Bring hands to the heart.*)

N: "Praise [God] for his mighty deeds;"

L and C: (*Bring hands to prayer position and kneel down.*)

N: "Praise [the Lord] according to his surpassing greatness!"

L and C: (*Bring hands outward to share blessings with everyone.*)

N: Now repeat after me . . . "Let everything that breathes. . . . "

L and C: "Let everything that breathes . . ."

N: "praise the Lord!"

L and C: "praise the Lord!"

N: "Let everything that breathes praise the Lord!"

L and C: "Let everything that breathes praise the Lord!"

N: "Praise the Lord!"

L and C: "Praise the Lord!"

N: "Praise [God] with trumpet sound; . . . with lute and harp!"

L: (*Signal children to pick up instruments and play a few moments, then stop.*)

N: "Praise [God] with tambourine and dance . . . with strings and pipe!"

L: (*Signal start and stop.*)

N: "Praise [God] with clanging cymbals . . . with loud clashing cymbals!"

L: *(Signal start and let the "music" continue for a bit longer this time, then signal to stop.)* Let's do that again, and have that be our prayer of praise to God today . . . *(signal music to start again, and let continue for as long as you can stand it!).* Amen!

—*Joyce S. Fong*

What God Wants!

Scripture: 2 Chronicles 31:5 (NIV)

Season/Sunday: Stewardship or any leading up to stewardship

Focus: This sermon focuses on the meaning of the tithe.

Experience: A visual experience of the tithe; what a tithe looks and feels like.

Arrangements: Ten large apples that can be placed in a line on a table facing the kids and congregation.

Leader:	Good morning everyone! This is stewardship season in the church. Stewardship season is the time when we talk about giving gifts to God. Listen to this verse from 2 Chronicles and say each part after me: The Israelites generously gave . . .
Children:	The Israelites generously gave . . .
L:	their grain, new wine, oil, and honey . . .
C:	their grain, new wine, oil, and honey . . .
L:	and all that the fields produced.
C:	and all that the fields produced.
L:	They brought a great amount . . .
C:	They brought a great amount . . .
L:	a tithe of everything . . .
C:	a tithe of everything . . .
L:	dedicated to the Lord.
C:	dedicated to the Lord.
L:	Very good! Well, the Israelites gave all sorts of things to the Lord, all that their fields produced. I don't know if the Israelites had any apples, but I brought some today. Let's count them:
L and C:	One, two, three . . . ten apples.
L:	Let's pretend that we are the Israelites and these are <u>our</u> apples. Now here is the question: If we are going

to do as the Israelites did, and bring our gifts to God, how many apples should we bring? How many out of these ten apples do we bring for a tithe?

C: Ten. Five.

L: Yes, ten is one possibility, five sounds like a good amount, who else would like to say?

C: All of them. Nine.

L: Okay, you say ten too, and you say nine—okay, that would leave one for you! Well, the truth is that a tithe isn't all ten of your apples, or even nine. Any more guesses?

C: Eight?

L: A tithe isn't eight of your apples either (*if the kids get into the swing of this they may work it down number by number to . . .*) One! That's right, a tithe, our way of saying thank you to God for giving us these apples to begin with, is to return one of our apples! Isn't that amazing? We want to give God more than one, but God only asks for one as our tithe. And you know what else? That leaves nine for you to eat and share with your family, and anyone else who is hungry! But all you need to give to God is one. Isn't that amazing?

C: Can I give God two?

L: Sure, you can give God two if you insist. And what's true about apples is true about money and everything. If you have ten dollars, how many dollars does God ask for?

C: One!

L: Right! That's the meaning of that funny little word in the verse we just read, the word "tithe." Remember we said that the Israelites brought a tithe of everything and dedicated it to the Lord? A tithe means a tenth, one in ten! Who would have thought we'd be learning math right here in church?! Let's have a prayer and thank God for giving us so much . . . (*prayer*).

—*Bob Sharman*

The Good Steward
(Part One)

Scripture: Luke 19:12-27

Season/Sunday: Stewardship/Thanksgiving. Note: this is the first part of a sermon that takes two Sundays to complete.

Focus: Luke's version of this familiar parable has each steward being given the same amount. God gives us gifts and trusts us to use them wisely.

Experience: To experience being given a gift and being trusted to do something positive with it.

Arrangements: You will need one dollar for each child (*or five dollars if you are either courageous or wealthy!*). It is even more effective if this gift can be from the church and perhaps given to the children by a recognized church leader, perhaps whoever is responsible for church finance or church missions.

Leader:	Good morning. This is a special season in the life of our church. Does anyone know what it is?
Children:	November. Thanksgiving. Stewardship.
L:	All those are right answers! Does anyone know what stewardship means?
C:	Being good stewards. Doing something good for others. Giving our offering.
L:	That's right. This is the time of year when we celebrate the gifts that God has given us, and we do something good with them for other people. You know, Jesus once told a story about a man who was very wealthy. One day he had to go away on a trip, and so he called his most trusted stewards and gave them each a portion of his wealth. He said to take care of it while he was away, to do something good with it until he returned. (*Note: there is no need to go into the harsh punishment of the steward who did nothing and yielded no return.*)

110

Well, today we're going to do that same thing. I'm
going to invite our Missions Elder and our Finance
Elder forward *(leaders come forward)*. Good morning Mr. Partida; good morning, Ms. Gunter. Ms.
Gunter, I believe you have some of last week's offering with you?

Finance Elder: I do. I have a dollar here for each and every child!

L: Really? That's exciting. What are you going to do
with it?

Finance Elder: I'm going to give it to Mr. Partida, to use for missions, to do something good for God with it *(passes
money to other leader)*.

L: And what mission project do you have in mind, Mr.
Partida?

Missions Elder: I've been approved by our committee to entrust
this money to these young stewards and to ask them
to do something good with this church money *(dis-
tributes money)*.

C: Cool!

L: Now, whose money is this?

C: Mine!

L: No, it's God's! And what we'd like all of you to do is
to take this dollar, talk with your parents, and do
something good with it. Then come back next week
and report what you have done. Okay?

C: Can we buy candy with it?

L: Yes, if you give the candy away to someone.
Remember, you're to do something good with this.
You can't spend it on yourself. Let's have a prayer
and ask God to guide us in how to be good stewards
. . . *(prayer)*.

—*Jeff Hutcheson*

111

The Good Steward (Part Two)

Scripture: Luke 19:12-27

Season/Sunday: Stewardship/Thanksgiving. Note: this is the second part of a sermon that takes two Sundays to complete.

Focus: Luke's version of this familiar parable has each steward being given the same amount. God gives us gifts and trusts us to use them wisely.

Experience: To hear the stories of what the children did with the money they received last week. There will, of course, be some children who were not present last week, and so theirs is a listening role. There may be some who did nothing with the gift they received and who have it with them. Have an offering plate handy to receive the gift back to the church.

Arrangements: You will need an offering plate, and if those who helped last week are available to come forward and hear the stories, so much the better. It would also be good to have a back-up plan in case no one has a story to tell. Either the leader or the Missions Elder could share a story or two of what the larger church has done in mission with some of the money it has received: a food or clothes closet, rent assistance or gas money given to someone in the community, money sent to an overseas missionary the church might support, and so on. The more personalized and detailed the better. Other ideas might also include calling on the choir director to show some music that was purchased, or asking a church school teacher to show some lesson materials (*be sure to arrange ahead of time*).

> **Leader:** I'd like to invite the children forward, and perhaps a parent would like to come with you to help tell us what you did with the dollar you got last week. If you didn't do anything with the dollar, and just want to bring it back here and put it in the offering plate, you can do that too! And if you weren't here last

week, just come forward anyway and listen to the stories!

Children: (*Tell their stories . . . they are sure to be quite inspiring!*)

L: Those were some wonderful stories! Let's have a prayer and give thanks that God has helped us be such good stewards . . . *(prayer).*

—Jeff Hutcheson

Follow the Light

Scripture: John 1:1-13

Season/Sunday: Advent

Focus: Jesus calls his followers to follow him as the light of the world.

Experience: To follow the light around the sanctuary and to experience the metaphor of Jesus being the Light of the world. To be a disciple is to follow Jesus Christ, who is the light.

Arrangements: You will need three flashlights—a tiny one, a regular-sized one, and the biggest one you can find—all in a bag. Arrange with an usher to turn off the lights in the sanctuary (*and otherwise make it as dark as possible*) on your cue. Also, think through the route you will take with the children and be prepared to carry on the discussion about Jesus Christ being our light for as long as necessary to arrive at your ending place (*which doesn't necessarily have to be the place where you started*). In fact, a nice way to end this sermon is by carrying the light out into the world, leading the children outside, just beyond the sanctuary doors!

> **Leader:** Good morning, everyone!
> **Children:** Hey!
> **L:** I brought something to show you this morning (*reach into your bag and pull out the tiny flashlight, turn it on, and shine it around*). Do you know what this is?
> **C:** A flashlight. I have a flashlight.
> **L:** That's right, this is a tiny flashlight. This tiny flashlight is a little light of mine and I'm gonna let it shine (*shine light around room*). Each one of us is like a little, wonderful beam of God's light. But what would we have if we put all of our little lights together?
> **C:** A bunch of lights.
> **L:** (*Reaching into bag and pulling out middle flashlight*) That's right. Put together all of our little lights, and

114

you get a bigger light. This light could represent our church light, when we all gather here and shine together. But did you know that we are all following an even bigger light? (*Pull out the biggest light of all.*)

C: Wow, that's the biggest flashlight I've ever seen!

L: The Bible calls Jesus the light of the world, and so following Jesus is following the biggest and best light of all! (*Cue usher to turn off light.*)
Come on, let's follow this light on a little trip around the sanctuary.

C: (*Follow.*)

L: (*Talking as you move around*) What are some of the good reasons for following the light of Jesus Christ?

C: You won't get lost. You can see. You know where to go.

L: Those are all great answers!

C: Jamie's not following the light. He is in front of it.

L: That's okay. He's still keeping his eye on it, and that's the most important thing, to keep our eyes following the light of Jesus Christ. And where are we going now (*having led children to church doors*)?

C: Outside!

L: That's right! Jesus asks us to follow him out into the world, and to take his light to people who don't have it. Let's have a prayer and ask Jesus to help us all keep our eyes on him . . . (*prayer*).

—*Jeff Hutcheson*

A Tight Fit

Scripture: Matthew 2:18-25; Luke 2:1-8; or Philippians 2:5-11

Season/Sunday: Advent or Christmas

Focus: The mystery of the incarnation is difficult to grasp. This sermon focuses on the size of God as one way to talk about the miracle of Jesus' coming in the flesh.

Experience: The children will work with the leader to fit increasingly larger packages into impossibly small containers.

Arrangements: A small gift bag or box and a Bible, both placed inside a slightly larger gift bag or box. Also, arrange with the mother of an infant to sit close down in front for interaction later. Secure the parent's permission to hold the child during the sermon.

Leader: *(As the children gather, be working to fit the Bible into the impossibly small gift bag or box. Once children have gathered, some will probably comment on the impossibility of the task; if not, solicit their input.)*
Do you think I'll ever get this Bible into this bag?

Children: NO! It's too small.

L: My bag is too small? Really? Well, that's okay; I have another idea. Come with me. *(Move to Communion table. Using larger gift bag or box, begin working to put Communion table into it.)* *(Grunting)* Urrhg, huuumph, hmm, is this table going to fit in here?

C: No! It's still too small.

L: Hmm. So maybe what I need are lots of containers, would that help?

C: Yes.

L: Okay, I've got another idea. Would each of you agree to be a container for me? Because what I really want to do is fit everything in the church into something.

116

So if I could put the pulpit in you *(indicate a child, and so throughout)*, and the table inside of you, and the cross in you . . . do you think that will work?

C: No! It's still too big.

L: Hmm. Well, I think what you're trying to tell me is that you can't put something really big into something small. Is that it?

C: Yes.

L: So I just want to make sure, are you telling me that you can't put a really, really big thing into a really, really small thing?

C: Yes.

L: You're sure?

C: Yes.

L: You're positive?

C: Yes!

L: *(Move to infant and invite children to follow, talking as you go.)* Okay, come over here with me. So, what's the biggest thing we know about?

C: The world. The universe. God.

L: Yup, I think God is the biggest One we can imagine *(take baby from mother)*. That's what makes the miracle of Christmas so completely amazing. Our big, huge God wanted to be near us so much that in Jesus Christ he got really, really small and came inside a baby to be near us. In fact, God didn't just come inside a baby, God became a baby, the baby Jesus. That was a tight fit! But God loves us so much, and wanted so much to be close to us, that it didn't matter. Let's have a prayer and thank God for this amazing, mysterious, miracle . . . *(prayer)*.

—*Brant D. Baker*

The First Gift

Scripture: Genesis 2:7

Season/Sunday: Advent

Focus: God gives us every good gift including God's first gift, the breath that sustains us.

Experience: To remember the first gift we ever received, and to experience again God's first gift.

Arrangements: A small empty gift box, gift-wrapped.

Leader: Good morning! How are you today?

Children: Good!

L: (*Displaying the gift box*) Christmas time is almost here. Are you ready?

C: Yea, I'm gonna get a bike.

L: It's fun to receive gifts, isn't it? I have one right here. Can you guess what's in it?

C: Money. A Bible.

L: Nope, it's not those. (*Shake it.*) Hmmm. It doesn't make any noise, and it's very light.

C: A feather.

L: Nope, not a feather. I'll give you a hint. It is the very first gift you ever received.

C: A doll?

L: No, it's not a doll. Let's open it and find out. (*Open the box and take a deep breath.*)

C: It's empty!

L: Oh no, it wasn't empty. It was the first gift I ever received, and the first gift you ever received (*take another deep breath*).

C: Air?

L: That's close. The first gift we ever receive is from God: a big deep breath (*inhale again and invite the children to breath deeply as well*). Let's have a prayer and thank God for every breath we take . . . (*prayer*).

—*Jeff Hutcheson*

118

A King Is Born!

Scripture: Matthew 2; Luke 2

Season/Sunday: Christmas

Focus: The children will learn that on this day a great king was born and his name was Jesus.

Experience: The children will hear the birth of Jesus from the perspective of animals. As they listen to the story, they will make sounds or actions corresponding to the following keywords heard.

> **Wise pig** – push nose up
> **Bird** – flapping hands
> **Hen** – wings and head in and out
> **Cow** – moo, moo
> **King** – bowing

Arrangements: This sermon works best if you have five helpers to read the animal lines and the leader to lead the respective motions. It may also help if you have highlighted the lines for each character as a cue to yourself to pause for the sounds and actions for each animal. Another possibility is to have one helper be the narrator of the story while the leader participates in the story with the children. If the children are young or the leader is worried about their ability to remember all of this, another possibility is to involve the entire congregation in the story. For instance, have the right side (or men) of the congregation be the birds, left side (or women) of the congregation be the cow, choir be the hens, children group 1 be the king, and children group 2 be the wise pig. The key to this sermon is be organized but most importantly have fun in celebrating the birth of Christ!

> **Leader:** Good morning, everyone! Today is a glorious day. Today we celebrate the birth of Jesus Christ. Many of you have heard the story of his birth before so I would like to have you help me with this story. Your

job is to listen to the story very carefully because every time I say the word "**wise pig,**" you have to push up your nose. Let me see everyone do that.

Children: (*Practice this action.*)

L: Good! When you hear me say, "**bird,**" flap your wings. Let me see everyone do that.

C: (*Practice this action.*)

L: When you hear me say, "**hen,**" make your chicken wings (*hands underneath armpits*) and pop your head in and out like a chicken. Let me see everyone do that.

C: (*Practice this action.*)

L: Good! When you hear me say "**cow,**" say "moo, moo." Let me hear everyone do that.

C: (*Practice this action.*)

L: That's super! Now this is the last one. When you hear me say "**king,**" bring your hands up high and bow down like you're bowing to a king. Let me see everyone do that.

C: (*Practice this action.*)

L: Wow, you are going to be great helpers! Let's see if you remember all the movements. (*Randomly call out the different characters: wise pig, bird, hen, cow, and king to see if the children have the motions/noise right. Also, encourage the congregation to join in!*) All right, I think we're ready for the story! One early morning, a **bird** flew in screaming, "The **king** is coming; the **king** is coming!"

The **wise pig** said, "Coming where?"

The **bird** said, "Here!"

The **hen** said, "Here in this manger?"

The **bird** screamed, "Yes, here to us, in the manger!"

The **cow** asked, "And how do you know this?"

The **bird** said, "I overheard the angel talking to the shepherds. It was amazing, with a choir of angels who sang a song more beautiful than my own. Then, on my way back, I overheard three smart-looking men say they were following a bright star, a star that would lead them to the **king.**"

The **wise pig** said, "She is right, for it was written by the prophet Micah: 'And you, Bethlehem, in the land of Judah, are by no means least among the rulers of Judah; for from you shall come a ruler who is to shepherd my people Israel.'"

The animals all said, "Then we must prepare the way for the coming of the **King**." So for that whole day the animals got ready. The **hen** swept the place clean. The **cow** cleaned her feeding box. The **wise pig** trampled the ground to make sure it was good for walking. The **bird** flew around outside to be on the lookout.

As night came, the **bird** screamed, "The **King** is here! The **King** is here!" The animals bowed low and watched as a man and a woman entered, dressed in shabby, ordinary clothes. The animals looked at each other confused.

The **bird** asked, "Hey, but where is the **King**?"

The **cow** said, "Shhhh . . . maybe he is following them. Maybe they're here to make sure the place is clean enough!"

The **hen** said, "Of course, it's clean!"

So the animals waited patiently. A few hours later, a strange thing happened. The woman gave birth to a baby boy, and she placed the baby boy in a feedbox. Then shepherds came and bowed before the child. Three smart-looking men came, bowed before the child, and gave him gifts of gold, frankincense, and myrrh.

The **bird** said, "I don't understand. Why are they bowing to the child?

The **cow** said, "A **king** is powerful and rich."

The **hen** said, "That child is small and poor."

Then the **wise pig** said, "The child is the **King**. He is the Son of God, our Messiah. His birth brings us good news of great joy for all the people and animals. He gives us hope because God has sent him to save us. His name is Jesus."

So all the animals believed. They bowed down before the child named Jesus. Let's have a prayer and thank God for how Jesus came to be with us . . . *(prayer— you might consider ending the prayer with the word "King").*

— *Joyce S. Fong*

Contributors

Brant D. Baker holds graduate degrees from Princeton Theological Seminary and Columbia Theological Seminary. He served churches in the southern United States prior to becoming senior pastor of First Presbyterian Church in Mesa, Arizona. Dr. Baker has written numerous books, including three on children's sermons. Two of his titles, *Play That Preaches* and *Teaching P.R.A.Y.E.R.*, are available from Abingdon Press. Brant is married and has two teenagers.

Joyce S. Fong is a special education teacher in New York City, teaching children with emotional disturbance in kindergarten through second grade. She has a master of arts in Christian education from Union Theological Seminary and Presbyterian School of Christian Education. Her focal interest is in children's ministry, and she has assumed varied roles, such as children's worship director, Sunday school teacher, and day camp codirector.

Kathleen Harris has lived in Arizona for eight years, where she serves as the Director of Children's Ministry at Valley Presbyterian Church in Paradise Valley. Prior to this she served as the Director of Christian Education at First Presbyterian Church in El Paso, Texas, the city in which she was born and raised. Kathleen is an ordained elder and deacon in the Presbyterian Church. Kathleen and her husband, Tom, have two children, Christopher and Ashley, who are both students at Arizona State University.

Paula Hoffman has worked with children and youth since 1978, as a youth evangelist and a certified Christian educator. She served congregations in Minnesota, Kansas, Oklahoma, and Georgia before attending seminary at

Columbia Theological Seminary in Decatur, Georgia. She is now pastor of First Presbyterian Church in Warner Robins, Georgia. She has published a children's musical, curriculum, and has written, but not published, the next great American novel. She plays guitar and piano, and shares her home with two feline roommates.

Jeff L. Hutcheson is pastor of the First Presbyterian Church of Cleveland, Georgia. He has also served congregations in Florida and Alabama. Jeff received a master of divinity from Columbia Theological Seminary, and also holds a master in psychology from Auburn University at Montgomery, Alabama. He continues to be an aspiring writer and is currently completing a Ph.D. in Human and Organizational Development. He lives in the "gateway to the mountains" with his wonderful wife, Sherri, and their two dogs, Chewy and Gizmo.

Benjamin Keller is a Presbyterian minister and author of several studies for children, youth, and adults, including curriculum for an international missions organization. He alternates his work between the parish ministry, primarily in the areas of Christian Education and Children's Ministry, and the hospital settings where he serves as a chaplain. He received his master of divinity from Dubuque Seminary in Iowa with an emphasis in Pastoral Theology and Congregational Care. He lives with his wife, Samantha, in Colorado and is an avid gourmet cook.

William Robert (Bob) Sharman III, a Presbyterian minister, has served churches in Alabama and Germany, where he served the American Protestant Church of Bonn. He presently serves as senior minister at Jamestown Presbyterian Church in Jamestown, North Carolina. A graduate of the University of Mississippi, Princeton Theological Seminary, and Columbia Theological Seminary, Dr. Sharman is committed to excellence in children's sermons. He is married, has three children and a golden retriever, and believes it is a terrific practice to rehearse children's sermons with your pet!

Scripture Index